CW00541115

World Wisdom
The Library of Perennial Philosophy

The Library of Perennial Philosophy is dedicated to the exposition of the timeless Truth underlying the diverse religions. This Truth, often referred to as the *Sophia Perennis*—or Perennial Wisdom—finds its expression in the revealed Scriptures as well as in the writings of the great sages and the artistic creations of the traditional worlds.

Songs without Names: Volumes I-VI appears as one of our selections in the Writings of Frithjof Schuon series.

The Writings of Frithjof Schuon

The Writings of Frithjof Schuon form the foundation of our library because he is the preeminent exponent of the Perennial Philosophy. His work illuminates this perspective in both an essential and comprehensive manner like none other.

Songs without Names

Volumes I-VI

Poems by

Frithjof Schuon

Foreword by
Annemarie Schimmel

Introduction by
William Stoddart

Translated from the German

World Wisdom

Songs without Names
Volumes I-VI
©2006 World Wisdom, Inc.

All rights reserved.
No part of this book may be used or reproduced
in any manner without written permission,
except in critical articles and reviews.

Library of Congress Cataloging-in-Publication Data

Schuon, Frithjof, 1907-1998
 [Poems. English. Selections]
 Songs without names, I-VI : poems / by Frithjof Schuon ; foreword by
Annemarie Schimmel ; introduction by William Stoddart.
     p. cm. — (The writings of Frithjof Schuon) (The library of perennial
philosophy)
 Includes index.
 ISBN-13: 978-1-933316-23-9 (pbk. : alk. paper)
 ISBN-10: 1-933316-23-3 (pbk. : alk. paper) 1. Schuon, Frithjof, 1907-1998.
Translations into English. 2. Religious poetry, German—20th century. I.
Title. II. Series. III. Series: Schuon, Frithjof, 1907-1998 Works. English. 2002.
 PT2680.U474A2 2006
 831'.92—dc22

                                                    2006011822

Cover: Frithjof Schuon
Photograph by Michael Pollack

Printed on acid-free paper in Canada

For information address World Wisdom, Inc.
P.O. Box 2682, Bloomington, Indiana 47402-2682

www.worldwisdom.com

Contents

Foreword   vii

Introduction   ix

Translator's Note   xvi

Songs without Names I   1

Songs without Names II   53

Songs without Names III   107

Songs without Names IV   153

Songs without Names V   203

Songs without Names VI   249

Notes   314

Index of Foreign Quotations   315

Index of First Lines   316

Foreword

It seems that mystical experience almost inevitably leads to poetry. The great mystics all over the world used the language of poetry when trying to beckon to a mystery that lies beyond normal human experience, and the most glorious works in Eastern and Western religions are the hymns of the mystics, be they Sufis or Christians, Hindus or Zen monks. Different as their expressions are, one feels that the poetical word can more easily lead to the mystery that is hidden behind the veils of intellectual knowledge and which cannot be fettered in logical speech.

In the world of Islam, the love-intoxicated poems of Maulana Jalaladdin Rumi are considered by many to be "the Koran in the Persian tongue," and Rumi is only one of many intoxicated souls who expressed their love and longing, and their experience of the Divine Unity, in verse. And even those mystics who preferred a more "intellectual" approach to the Absolute couched their experiences in verse. The prime example is, of course, Ibn Arabi whose *Tarjuman al-ashwaq* translated his experience of the One, Unattainable Deity into the language of traditional Arabic poetry.

Taking this fact into consideration we are not surprised that Frithjof Schuon too felt compelled to write poetry—and, it is important to note, poetry in his German mother tongue. His verse sometimes reflects ideas and images of R. M. Rilke's *Stundenbuch*, in which the expert on mysticism can find some strange echoes of Ibn Arabi's ideas. This may be an accident, for mystical ideas are similar all over the world; but the German reader of Schuon's verses enjoys the familiar sound. This sound could not be maintained in the English translations of his poetry. Yet, as he himself explains, what really matters is the content, and here we listen to the thinker who, far from the intricate and complex scholarly sentences of his learned prose works, sings the simple prayers of the longing soul: God is the center, the primordial ground which comprehends everything, manifesting Himself through the colorful play of His creations. And it is the human heart which alone can reflect the incomprehensible Being, for humanity's central quality is divinely inspired love, which is the axis of our life.

I hope that Schuon's mystical verse will be read not only by English speaking readers but even more by those who understand German.[1] They will enjoy many of these tender lyrics which show the famous thinker in a very different light and from an unexpected side.

—Annemarie Schimmel, Professor Emeritus, Harvard University

---

[1] See Translator's Note on page *xvi*

Introduction

Frithjof Schuon (1907-1998) was a sage, an artist, and a poet. During the last three years of his life, he wrote in German—his mother tongue—approximately 3,500 short poems, in 23 separate collections. In content, Schuon's German poems are similar to those in his English collection *Road to the Heart*, but they are much more numerous, and the imagery is even more rich and powerful. The poems cover every possible aspect of metaphysical doctrine, spiritual method, spiritual virtue, and the role and function of beauty. They express every conceivable subtlety of spiritual and moral counsel—and this not merely in general terms, but with uncanny intimacy, detail, and precision. They exhibit incredible sharpness, profundity, comprehensiveness, and compassion. They are his final gift to the world, his testament and his legacy.

Some of the poems are autobiographical, with reminiscences of places experienced: Basle and Paris, the fairy-tale streets of old German towns, Morocco and Andalusia, Turkey and Greece, the American West. Others evoke the genius of certain peoples, such as the Hindus, the Japanese, the Arabs, the Red Indians, and also the Cossacks and the Gypsies. Yet other poems elucidate the role of music, dance, and poetry itself. In one or two poems, the godless modern world comes in for biting, and sometimes fiercely humorous, comment:

> *Ein weltlich Fest: Lampenkristalle schimmern*
> *Im großen Saal —*
> *Und glänzende Gesellschaft, Damen, Herrn,*
> *Sitzen beim Mahl.*
> *Man spricht von allem und man spricht von nichts —*
> *Der Wein ist rot,*
> *Und so der Blumenschmuck.*
> *Doch keiner, keiner*
> *Denkt an den Tod.*

A worldly banquet: chandeliers glitter
In the large hall —
And brilliant society, ladies and gentlemen

Sit down for the meal.
They talk of everything and they talk of nothing —
The wine is red,
And so are the flowers.
                              But no one, no one
Thinks of death.

(*Stella Maris*, "The Celebration")

The poems embody both severity and compassion. They are powerfully interiorizing. Their content epitomizes Schuon's teaching, which he himself has summarized in the words Truth, Prayer, Virtue, and Beauty. For him, these are the four things needful; they are the very purpose of life, the only source of happiness, and the essential means of salvation. The poems convey these elements to the reader not only mentally, but also, as it were, existentially; their role is both doctrinal and sacramental.

The central role of prayer is powerfully expressed in the following poem entitled "*Panakeia*" ("panacea," the remedy for all ills):

Warum hat Gott die Sprache uns geschenkt?
Für das Gebet.
Weil Gottes Segen dem, der Ihm vertraut,
Ins Herze geht.

Ein Beten ist der allererste Schrei
in diesem Leben.
So ist der letzte Hauch ein Hoffnungswort —
Von Gott gegeben.

Was ist der Stoff, aus dem der Mensch gemacht,
Sein tiefstes Ich?
Es ist das Wort, das uns das Heil gewährt:
Herr, höre mich!

Why has God given us the gift of speech?
For prayer.
Because God's blessing enters the heart of him
Who trusts in God.

The very first cry in this life
Is a prayer.

And the last breath is a word of hope —
　　　Given by God.

What is the substance of which man is made,
　　　His deepest I?
It is the Word that grants us salvation:
　　　Lord, hear me!

(Stella Maris, "Panacea")

Many of the poems express the purpose of life with unmistakable clarity, for example:

Jedes Geschöpf ist da, um "Gott" zu sagen;
So musst auch du der Welt Berufung tragen,
O Mensch, der du der Erde König bist —
Weh dem, der seines Daseins Kern vergisst;

Dies tut nicht Tier noch Pflanze, ja kein Stein;
Dies tut der willensfreie Mensch allein
In seinem Wahn.
　　　　　Sprich "Gott" in deinem Wandern;
Es werde eine Gnade für die Andern.

Denn eine Aura strahlt vom Höchsten Namen —
Gebet ist Segen, ist der Gottheit Samen.

All creatures exist in order to say "God";
So must thou too accept the world's vocation,
O man, who art king of the earth —
Woe unto him who forgets the kernel of his existence;

No animal, no plant nor stone does this;
But only man, with his free will,
In his madness.
　　　　　Say "God" throughout thy life;
It will be a grace for others too.

For an aura radiates from the Supreme Name —
Prayer is blessing; it is the seed of the Divine.

(Stella Maris, "The Aura")

But the dread consequences of a wrong choice are not forgotten:

In Indien sagt man oft, dass Japa-Yoga
Stets Segen bringe — dass das Rāma-Mantra
Ein Wundermittel sei, das helfen müsse.
Dem ist nicht so, denn zürnen kann Shrī Rāma.

In India it is often said that *Japa-Yoga*
Always brings blessings — that the *Rāma-Mantra*
Is a miraculous means, that cannot but help.
This is not so, for Shrī Rāma can also show His wrath.

(Songs without Names I-XXXIII)

Und Gottes Zorn — er war zuvor schon da;
Denn Gottes Nein begleitet Gottes Ja.
Ihr fragt: war Gott zuerst nicht reine Milde?
Des Zornes Möglichkeit war auch im Bilde.

And God's anger — it was already there;
For God's No accompanies God's Yes.
You ask: is God not first and foremost Mercy?
The possibility of anger is also in the picture.

(Songs without Names II-LXXII)

Das Gottgedenken muss den Menschen ändern,
Denn zum Beleuchten gibt die Lampe Licht;
Wenn unsre Seele nicht verbessert wird,
Dann zählt das Sprechen frommer Formeln nicht.

Lass ab von falscher Größe — werde klein
Und selbstlos, und du wirst im Himmel sein.

God-remembrance must change man,
For the purpose of a lamp is to give light;
If our soul is not improved,
Then reciting pious formulas is of no avail.

Renounce false greatness — become small
And selfless, and thou wilt be in Heaven.

(Songs without Names IV-II)

Our human smallness is exposed without pity:

Lärmendes Nichts ist manche Menschenseel —
Was bläht sie sich, als wär sie gottgeboren?
Ein kurzer Erdentraum voll Eitelkeit,
Ruhloses Tun — und alles ist verloren.

Besinnet euch: seid klein, denn Gott ist groß.
Er hat euch eine Heimat zubereitet
Im Himmelreich: ein goldner Zufluchtsort —
Wohl dem, der gegen seine Seele streitet!

Many a human soul is a noisy void —
Why is she inflated as if born of God?
A brief earthly dream, full of vanity,
Restless activity — and all is lost.

Remember: be small, for God is great.
He has prepared for you a homeland
In the Kingdom of Heaven, a golden shelter —
Blessèd is he who fights against his soul!

(*Adastra*, "Smallness")

Again and again, the poems return to the perplexing and agonizing problem of evil:

Da wo das Lichte erscheinet,
Da muss auch das Finstere drohen;
Wundre und gräme dich nicht;
So will es das wirkende Sein.
Siehe, die niederen Mächte
Bekämpfen heimtückisch die hohen;
Da wo ein Abel erstrahlet,
Da ist auch ein finsterer Kain.

Denn die Allmöglichkeit Gottes
Erfordert ja auch die Verneinung:
Wahrheit und Friede sind himmlisch,
Irdisch sind Falschheit und Krieg.
Ohne das Übel der Trennung,
Wo wäre das Gut der Verneinung?

Ohne der Finsternis Treiben,
        Wo wäre der Trost und der Sieg?

Wherever light appears
        Darkness must also threaten;
Do not wonder and grieve,
        Existence will have it thus.
See how the lower powers
        Maliciously battle the higher;
Wherever Abel shines,
        There also is dark Cain.

For God's All-Possibility
        Also demands negation:
Truth and Peace are of Heaven,
        Earthly are falsehood and war.
Without the evil of separation,
        Where would be the good of reunion?
Without the work of darkness,
        Where would be solace and victory?

                    (*Adastra*, "Cosmos")

No translation can possibly do full justice to the "poetry"—the meter, rhyme, verbal appositeness, allusions, music, inspiration—of the original German. Each German poem is a diamond—sparkling and clear, an architectural masterpiece full of light.

In his rich profusion of references to the many and varied cultural forms of Europe and beyond—the streets of the Latin Quarter, Andalusian nights, the Virgen del Pilar, the Macarena, sages such as Dante, Shankara, Pythagoras and Plato, the Psalms of David, Arab wisdom, the graces of the Bodhisattvas, Tibetan prayer-wheels, Samurai and Shinto, the songs of love and longing of many peoples—in all of these diverse cultures, Schuon captures the timeless message of truth and beauty which each contains, and renders it present in a most joyful way. When these cultural forms happen to be ones that the reader himself has known and loved, the joy that emanates from the poems is great indeed.

Schuon's long cycle of poems has already been compared to Rumi's *Mathnāwī*. I think that many of his poems can also be compared to the Psalms of David: they are an expression of nostalgia, of mankind's longing for, and ultimate satisfaction in, the Lord. Their main theme is trustful prayer to an ever-merciful God, and benevolence towards men of goodwill. First and foremost, the poems are instruments of instruction. As such, they are a powerful propulsion towards the inward.

A blessing lies not only in the quality of the poems, but also in the quantity—they constitute an all-inclusive totality. On the one hand, Schuon's German poems recapitulate the teachings contained in his philosophical works in French; on the other, they are an inexhaustible, and ever new, purifying fountain—a crystalline and living expression of the *Religio perennis*. They epitomize truth, beauty, and salvation.

—William Stoddart

Translator's Note

Schuon considered his poems didactic in nature and termed them "Sinngedichte," or teaching poems. With this in mind, the aim of the present English edition is to provide a literal rendering of the German text that remains as true as possible to the author's meaning. These translations are the work of William Stoddart, in collaboration with Catherine Schuon and Tamara Pollack. The translations draw extensively on Schuon's own informal, dictated translations. For a full appreciation of the lyrical resonance and musicality of the original, the reader is referred to the several German editions of these poems currently available.[1]

The last nineteen of these twenty-three collections are grouped under two primary headings, *Songs without Names I-XII* and *World Wheel I-VII*. The chronological order in which these collections were written, spanning three years from 1995-1998, is as follows: *Adastra, Stella Maris, Autumn Leaves, The Ring, Songs without Names I-V, World Wheel I, Songs without Names VI-XII*, and *World Wheel II-VII*.

---

[1] The complete German text of these poems is available in ten volumes from Editions Les Sept Flèches, 1062 Sottens, Suisse, www.sept-fleches.com, as a bilingual German/French edition. A complete bilingual German/Spanish edition is in preparation for 2007 from José J. de Olañeta, Editor, Palma de Mallorca, Spain. Selections can also be found in: *Liebe, Leben, Glück*, and *Sinn* (Freiburg im Breisgau: Verlag Herder, 1997); *Songs for a Spiritual Traveler* (Bloomington: World Wisdom, 2002); and *Adastra & Stella Maris: Poems by Frithjof Schuon* (Bloomington: World Wisdom, 2003).

Songs without Names

First Collection

Why are these songs without names?
The poet wrote them down as they came;
He did not want them — they wanted him;
Who knows when they will end at the Lord's behest.

Fundamentally each aphorism conveys the same message —
Symbols can meet and unite.

Songs without Names

First Collection

I

Birth, and then death — this is one thing.
Separation through the force of destiny — this is another.
Between the two, life's long struggle;
And God's Word: think of Me and go thy way upward
On the sacred Path, from thee to Me.

See: life's poles are the frame
For a path leading from illusion to the True:
A path from the dream of life to the Self, to the "We."

II

Ye think that there are human collectivities,
Historical relationships; how so?
In reality, there are only individual souls,
Dream-veils — individual joys, individual pains.

Ye are born into a world.
And ye take it seriously: history seems important —
But ye forget that one must die alone.
The coming of God reduces the illusion to ashes.

III

Cogito ergo sum — the fact that humans think
Is not a proof, but it is a sign
Of the Most High. He who needs proof
Will never reach Truth's meaning or its Being.

Immortality: because God, the Most High, is.
Ye doubt, because ye know not that ye know.

IV

Not only revelation, but also experience teaches us:
There exists on earth a heavenly Power
That can help, and with which we may talk;
Which sternly but kindly watches over our actions.
This is certain; even though the earthly world
Is divided into good and evil.

There are the people who love or hate each other.
Theòs estin — we are not abandoned.

V

In the beginning was the Word, which created all things —
Then there is the heart, wherein the Most High dwells.
This is man's meaning and his happiness —
Understand, O man, that creation is worthwhile.

VI

Here-below and hereafter — two different worlds,
Not only as earth and Heaven, but also
In this earthly life: the outward and the inward —
Refuge in the inward is the wise man's way.

The question is where my I is to be found:
Among men, where I must dream —
Or in the Sign that links us to God.

VII

Paradox: we are in earthly life
For the purpose, inversely, of striving toward Heaven:
We have been imprisoned in Nature's law,
So that we may transcend it.

The meaning of existence? Why dig for wisdom,
When it can only have this one meaning?

VIII

All-Possibility: from it stem the many things
That we see in the world and in life;
All destiny's colors, joys and pains,
In *Māyā's* unfathomable play.

See the colorful splendor of the many birds:
Here are the red ones, there the blue and yellow.
God did not make us from without —
Each living being willed itself.

God said: I was a Treasure, but no one knew
Of It; then came the world, which had to know Me.

IX

Certitude is Being, when it is reflected
In the uncertain space of our thought;
Being reflects itself therein because this space calls it —
A longing call out of its earthly dream.

Thought's longing is its essential content —
Thought summons Being, its own self — come soon!

X

I would like to stand before the sun,
Conscious that before God it is a grain of sand,
Or a nothingness. And this is important:
I see the sun, but it does not see me —
So know, O man: it is not what thou art.

Never mind if they call thee a heathen:
The sun is the true image of Divinity.

XI

A wise man said: ask yourselves — who am I?
This is not a Path. The wise man meant himself,
Describing his spiritual substance, given by God;
But it is not your substance, simply because ye think the same.

One cannot, without God, reduce the world to ashes —
'By its fruit ye shall recognize the spirit.'

XII

Thou hurriest along a path following thy desire;
Someone calls: stop! Thou standest as if spellbound —
Thus it is when, in the midst of thy dream,
The Spirit pronounces the Name Most High.

Thou stoppest, thou rememberest what thou art —
What Being, the meaning of all things, is.

The Spirit, like an arrow, flies into the All —
Or, like a crystal, it stands still in Being.

XIII

You ask me how the soul should be molded
In order to attain the highest goal.
The fundamental law — all pious people know —
Is pure intention and humility; and then prayer.

It comes from God and it has many levels —
The deepest prayer is the call of our heart.

Say not that thou art at the end of the Path;
Ungraspable is the goal, Infinity —
And thus endless; and divinely more than what thou knowest.

XIV

When one combines the All with the naught,
One has the rhythm that bears witness to both:
Meander of prayers, tremor of the heart,
Combines God and world and constitutes life.

XV

There is no need to describe water
When someone is thirsty — so said a pious man;
Water must be drunk — syllogisms
Are worthless, they cannot reach God.

People may believe this, but it is wrong
If it means that thought is useless
For realization. Without a keen mind,
God will not give us the highest lights.

Truth is clarity, it is the highest place —
Does not the Scripture say: "In the beginning was the Word."

XVI

Truth is everything. Altruism is
The hobby-horse of many mystics,
For whom the "I" is sin as such; and hail
To the error if the "I" has been hit!

"There is no right but that of Truth" —
Love of Truth is the beauty of the soul.

XVII

I am too tired to think of God,
Someone complained, I have no more strength,
What should I do? What shouldst thou do?
Thou shouldst repose in the fragrance of far-off God-remembrance.

Just as the *pariah*, who did not dare
To enter the sanctuary, nevertheless became blessed,
Because from afar he contemplated the temple's roof.

XVIII

What does the *Mea Culpa* mean?
Not that I am the worst of sinners;
It means that evil touches my soul;
May God help me — He is mighty, free.

Why then "my fault?" On both feet
Stand fast! Thou shouldst close thyself to the evil one.
The *Culpa* can also be in a man's very substance;
The *Mea Culpa* shows: he can be cured.

And may God grant that even on this earth
Ejaculatory prayer may still become a *Felix Culpa*.

XIX

Obligation is compulsion — unfree, but also free;
Free obligation is necessary willing.
When duty is in harmony with the impulse of love,
Then to act is a pleasure — without the gods being angry.

XX

Why was Solomon so misunderstood?
He was the temple builder — and more than that:
He was the wise man to whom Balkis journeyed —
And who had temples built to all the gods.

The essence was censured by the form —
Its advocate had plowed the ground too deeply.
The Bible wishes to speak to the average man —
If thou seekest the kernel, thou must break the shell.

XXII

Old men, they say, are of sad disposition;
A butterfly delights a little child,
So why should not the same delight the old?
And cannot the little child also be sad?

I am not trying to invent paradoxes —
Both could have good reasons for both moods.

XXIII

Let me greet the deep and wild forest —
A winding path down to a brook;
Deeply carved is the dark valley —

You hear how a birdsong fades away,
And sit on a tree stump,
Alone and in contemplation. Quiet hours —

You climb back up, hesitating through the brush,
On a trail that winds up to the light.

Forest: sanctuary of wilderness — nature
Whispers its secret in the tracks of Divinity.

XXIV

Suddenly snow came to my forest.
The landscape is no longer of this world —
Everywhere is the heavenly crystal,
On meadow, bush and tree, as far as eye can see.

The forest was life and also a sanctuary
With God's Presence. Now it is silence —
Neither death nor life, but the scent of eternity —
A timeless blessing shines from every branch.

XXV

One can endlessly torment oneself with problems —
To this chief problem, the following can be said:
Thou standest before the face of thy Creator;
Say: God! — And look! The problems are no more.

XXVI

Things past — of what use are they still?
I can only lean on experience.
Much was beautiful, but everything has turned to dust —
All that is good is preserved in God.

Since I am an I, I cannot but carry
Many images in my mind.
I should not pay attention to every image —
Rather I should drown many of them in oblivion.

The Creator — and He alone — knows best
Who I was, am, and should be.

XXVII

What God has given thee has its intrinsic worth —
And beauty has nourished thy poor heart.
Experience has often pushed thee aside,
But do not be angry —

                it shows the way upward.

XXVIII

All in all: most poets
Are judges of their own souls.
They wish to win over the outward world —
They see not the inward message of things.
Their narcissistic feelings have no limits —
They lose themselves in a morass of subtleties
And suffer from ephemeralities,
Instead of preparing their way to the All-Merciful.
Then comes the end, one knows not why —
Indifferent death turns the page.

XXIX

First Truth, then patience. The one
Satisfies your God-given intellect;
The other is yourselves. The one is
The Light of the Most High, the other is our life.

Light, life. Light — one should drink it,
For one should become what one really is.
Life, one accepts, from hour to hour;
To go one's way — yet not to drown in the world's naught.

XXX

Certitude of God is also certitude of salvation,
And to resignation belongs trust;
As thou see'st around thee the beauty of the world,
Thou shouldst at the same time look inwards.

If thou see'st in thy mind the image of God,
Then understand that the world bears witness to the Most High —
And that the inward, like the outward,
Bows down before the Sovereign Good.

XXXI

The essential thou shouldst always see;
Hence, the essential thou shouldst always do.
The essential thou shouldst always hear;
And in the essential thou shouldst repose.

So, day and night, remember
What the meaning of thine existence is.
Towards the highest Truth, that willed thee,
Thy soul should ever strive.

XXXII

Where does the path of science lead?
It is finally too much for man's strength.
The Titans sought to reach the sky —
"By their fruits ye shall know them."

You should not peer into the abysses of the universe,
This will end by obstructing your path to salvation.
Praised be the green meadow of this earth —
From it starts the path to Paradise.

The Creator willed that we be men —
We are children of both earth and Heaven.

XXXIII

In India, it is often said that *Japa-Yoga*
Always brings blessings — that the *Rāma-Mantra*
Is a miraculous means that cannot but help.
This is not so, for Shrī Rāma can also show His wrath;

The fault lies in man, and not in *Japa's* sweetness.
But God is free, and good in His nature —
What He decides, only He knows.

XXXIV

The Greek meander represents life,
With its to and fro: its outward, its inward —
It is Yin and Yang, but in duration;
This is how the Fates spin our destiny.

A twofold movement, endlessly repeated,
This is the meander's meaning — a constant oscillation.
Firstly: the intellect contemplates Being as such,
Then it also sees Being in things.

XXXV

The chain shows us how the forms of existence
Forever interlock, link by link;
Nothing on earth stands alone by itself;
He is wise who sees the wholeness of things.

The world and time — a never-ending meander,
Alternately uniting and separating;
The world should appear to thee as One in all —
And, conversely, all in One.

XXXVI

Vertical line and horizontal line —
Synthesis and analysis; the latter is secondary
To the former. Those whose thinking is immersed in multiplicity
Stress the analytical point of view.

Synthesis seeks to put illusion aside;
Analysis seeks to encompass everything.

Certitude, and from it, serenity:
This is the soul, and the measure of things.

All in One and One in All: this is
The sign of the cross that measures the universe.

XXXVII

Horizontal and vertical. Animals walk horizontally;
Man — so it seems — walks vertically.
His heart walks horizontally — this is his betrayal
Of the human state; he closes the door on himself.

There are also animals that like to stand vertically —
A play of nature, as if by mistake.

XXXVIII

So many people are but fragments, pieces,
But God intended man to be a whole.
God's image cannot be a fragment —
Man should remain as the Lord made him.

The more man cleaves to his ego,
The more he constricts and impoverishes himself.
Knowledge, devotion, noble character and
A sense of beauty make the soul complete.

It is astonishing how seriously people take themselves
In their illusions, amidst the perils of this life —
Not seeing how small false greatness is;
Cervantes saw through the whole farce.

XXXIX

There was a child whose toy was broken —
It seemed to him as if the world had come to an end.
The child did not remain a child, he became a man —
He no longer had any desire for that toy.

Thus it is with life and with the world —
Blessèd is he whose heart contains something infinitely higher.

XL

The city of Paris was the love of my youth —
The old streets near Notre Dame;
Dream-wanderings full of longing songs —
There it was that Heaven's grace came,
In a small room, under the roof —
It was there that a call from the Most High awoke in me.

And then came Africa — God let destiny
Weave several lives into my existence.

XLI

The town of Mostaghanem: dark blue sea,
A golden land with palm trees — and the mosque;
A few white houses. Pious people clad in white.
Then yellow sand, as far as eye can see.

The dervish brothers, who look toward the inward;
The holy Shaikh, to whom I had been brought.
Static dances and long litanies —
Radiant days; clear, star-filled nights.

XLII

Blue means depth, contemplativity;
Red means intensity and fervor;
Yellow is joy, a ray of happiness;
Then there are innumerable combinations.

The web of the world — made of forms, colors, and sounds —
Wants to divide, and yet to reconcile.
Earth's splendor testifies to the celestial —
The world is made of the footprints of the gods.

XLIII

If thou see'st the beautiful, which enraptures the soul,
Do not think it mere vanity and illusion;
Think that God is radiating His Nature —
The world partakes in the ardor of His Love.

Then think of the Essence, look inward —
And thou wilt gain beauty's eternity.
When praying, dream not of the earthly beautiful —
The soul should grow accustomed to death.

Tashbīh, Tanzīh: emptiness after fullness,
So say the Sufis. After the image, comes silence.

XLIV

When the soil was fertile,
Primordial man had no reason for hunting;
When there was game in prairie and wood,
He did not have to burden himself tilling the ground.

Ask not which of the two is better,
Both hunter and farmer have their nobility.
Each was priest, each stood before God —
God's blessing alone do I call wonderful.

Whether thou art farmer or hunter,
What makes thee noble, is what thou know'st of the Most High.

XLV

The eagle feather, a Red Indian said,
Means the presence of the Great Spirit:
The face of our heroes is surrounded
By a circle of feathers that lifts us up to the sun.

The Red priest holds an eagle feather,
Or an eagle fan, in order to bless
Or to chastise; he who is touched by this lofty sign,
May encounter the power of Heaven.

XLVI

The Spirit-Wheel: a symbol in the region
Of the Bighorn Mountains, in Crow country;
A wheel of stones laid out on the grass,
Where once stood a messenger from Heaven.

An image of the Sun Dance: axis, rim;
A magic that lifts up earth to Heaven.
The wise man brought the sacred down to earth,
So that man's heart could become a sun.

XLVII

From the horse comes that kind of soul
That one finds amongst proud, riding peoples;
Mongols, Red Indians, and Cossacks —
Men for whom earth's heaviness has disappeared.

Early or late, man became brother
To a noble animal that returns his love;
Beyond the burden of trudging on the earth,
The rider dreams of becoming an eagle.

Fearless racing, combat and proud singing —
There is a station that is even higher:
When thy soul feels the nearness of God,
And forgets itself in God-remembrance.

XLVIII

Although I am indebted to Shankara,
I take pleasure in the music of Spain,
Russia, the Gypsies, and the Red Indians —
What is the profound meaning of this contrast?

Extremes meet; and not only as regards forms —
The dance-song is the vehicle of deep insight.

XLIX

The Bible gave precedence to those who plant,
And not to those who hunt. The Jews were farmers
And, at the same time, God's people. Their worship
Eventually took place within a temple's walls.

But a building too is something transient —
Only the dark Wailing Wall remains.
And yet the last stone of the ruin
Can convey blessings and be a temple.

And so: the last breath of the Revelation
Contains the whole, just as does the smoke of the sacrifice.
The name "God," if one had nothing else,
Contains the entire soul of man.

L

What paradises are — one knows well;
For one has read about it in various Holy Scriptures.
But how the many miracles may be —
Who can lift the enigma's veil?

What does it matter if the Scriptures conceal many things?
The meaning of the heavenly world is bliss;
And it is certain, since we can perceive
The true nature of things in the depth of our heart.

If only we knew that deep in our heart
Paradise is calling us to fulfillment!

LI

The immense river of the whole Veda
Lies in the one sacred syllable *Om.*
Say *Om,* said Shankara — what more dost thou wish?
In the smallest drop of water is the sea.

LII

The universe is a measureless book
In which the mysteries of all beings are inscribed;
One knows them mostly by hearsay;
The eye of the heart can solve the enigmas.

It has often been said that deductions made by reason
Do not reach what the gaze of the heart can see;
Yet thinking may awaken this gaze,
If one protects the mind from error.

It is foolish to despise syllogisms —
It is essential that our heart should see.

LIII

In Japan, one calls *tomoye* a circle
In which three round fields intertwine.
A threefold yin-yang: yellow, red and green —
The world playfully divides itself into three zones.

So also the microcosm: our spirit,
Which radiates, glows and rests — three existential rays,
Each of which points to the Tao.

LIV

The white man's starting point is clear thinking,
Whereby the light of the mind may reach the goal.
The yellow man starts from experience,
Then comes the light; the goal is the same.

The white man hears; the yellow man sees;
Both are philosophers, in different garbs.
The word of the first: dialectic and music;
The word of the second: a look into nature.

We like the fullness of long didactic poems —
The East-Asian loves the stillness of a landscape.

LV

Why did the Red Indians always fight one other?
Why did the Samurai also do the same?
For reasons of virility: let no one think
That a proven man is like a woman.

The *kali-yuga* is what it is —
Ye should not blame the inevitable.
The fact is that in our times
No better way was found to show that one is a man.

Totally other is the question as to the nature
Of the holy war: this is the fight against evil.

LVI

Is it not strange that in Antiquity
The world was so heartless — what is the meaning
Of cruel customs? The ancient law of sacrifice:
Because repayment seemed to be the will of the gods.

In later times it became apparent
That the most agreeable sacrifice is the soul —
The strength of love that gives itself to the Most High.

Certainly, the sages already knew this —
But the general faith was drenched in blood.

God said: the best is that ye remember Me!

LVII

Be not surprised that Krishna, Abraham,
Moses and Mohammad, who brought blessings,
Were also warriors, despite their gentle dispositions;
They had to be harsh in a world of harshness.

The wisest Messenger cannot save
The wicked against their will.

LVIII

Even the sages who did not condemn harshness —
They let the guardians of the law prevail —
Declared: purer than the Ganges is the river
Of Truth — the best sacrifice is "Om."

LIX

It is said that fear alone maintains the world —
That threat prevents it from falling apart;
Sad enough. But forget not faith,
Lest the law should pierce man's heart.

Have faith first! Good men must suffer
Under the bad; but both should be helped.

If one wishes to help the one and the other,
One must rely on God's saving Word.

LX

It is said: in pain shall woman give birth;
Does this mean that God indulges her husband?
By the sweat of his brow he has to plow;
He loses his life in senseless wars.

It is true: a curse lies over this sinful earth —
Each sex has its own burden.

LXI

If something makes thee suffer, then think
That God is calling thee to think of Him;
He wishes thee to be in His proximity
As He is in thine; He does not wish to hurt thee.

LXII

The strength of the bad, the weakness of the good —
Who would suspect their interplay?
History demonstrates the guilt of both —
For the sins of both, the world is perishing.

What is called good, is relative:
There are those who resist evil,
But do so too late; when they cry out for help,
They are soon overrun by evil.

Strength is something that demons too may have;
In the good, strength takes the form of virtue.

LXIII

Say not that man may see God only in trials —
For the wise, joy too means God's proximity.
Think not that in happiness grace eludes thee —
In pleasure too, the Lord calls thee to Himself.

LXIV

What is nobility of soul, in the absence of which
Ye drink but poison, albeit from a consecrated cup?
It is the profound wish to perceive the essence
Of things, and God's activity in the world.

In this lies the death of the lower instincts —
Yet also a resurrection: love of God.

LXV

It is astonishing how the manner of expressing the truth
Can deviate even on the part of "knowers";
The reason is that, in spite of their capacity for knowing,
They do not know the art of complete thinking.

You may say that waking and dream are both illusions —
The question here is in which respect
You perceive *Māyā*'s illusion;
You do not have a lease on the essence of truth.

For everything depends on the particular viewpoint that is
The principle of your perception. So do not think
That one can promote the relatively true
As if it were the metaphysically certain.

If you think that the universe is within us, or that it is the
product of our thinking —
Then I cannot give you my attention.
Understand that I wish to be spared anything further.

LXVI

Naïve expressions often carry a deep meaning;
To pierce through the literal form can be worthwhile.
So strive toward the true intention;
Sages do it. But not epigones.

LXVII

I think, but I do not brood;
If it seems that I do, it is simply because I clarify
What is obscure for others. Truth is clear
In itself; divine doctrine is crystalline.

We teach what we must, and what we love.
The limits of speech are written in God.

LXVIII

"Double truth," was the Medieval term:
Theology was for all, for the multitude;
Philosophy, as it was called, was for those
Who saw further than the narrowness of dogma,
And yet held firmly to their faith —
On its plane, and within the limits of the law.

In popular speech it is said: thoughts pay no taxes —
God gives us naked Truth, without wavering.

LXIX

To think is natural; unnatural
It is to think too much in too short a time,
For the mind must rest; not out of self-indulgence
Or laziness, but in order that it may give all the more.

Our capacity for thought is not a possession
Of our own; it is consecrated to the Lord,
It has no meaning, and no right, apart from Him;
The goal of thinking is Eternity.

LXX

God; the prophet; my "I." These are the three mysteries
With which every pious man must live.
The "I" is the created gaze towards what is Above;
And in the prophet is the greeting of the Most High.

In God both poles are profoundly contained —
They had to unfold His Light towards the earth.

LXXI

Mystery of patience: the sorrow and vexation
That our weary soul must bear
Through the river of hours, through the river of days —
And each day has its own affliction.

Patience: nourished by an inner source
That knows no time; solace ever present,
Bestowed from Within — from Above;
Light is the burden — let God carry what is too heavy.

LXXII

Mary is the image of the seven sorrows;
But she is also the image of God's joy.
She is the archetype and model of our soul:

Archetype, because she is purity; and therefore
Model: holy patience on every path.

Mary is the lotus: she contains the divine child —
And with him the whole universe.

LXXIII

A symbol is the water lily
Which opens itself up to receive Heaven —
As if this recipient of the celestial rays
Itself wished to reach the luminous kingdom of Heaven.

A symbol is the swan, the companion of this flower —
Snow-white, it glides o'er the water's surface;
O may the soul, freed from idle passion,
Ever remain its archetype on the waters of life!

LXXIV

Someone was vexed and downcast —
Both outwardly and inwardly; many things
For which he had toiled, had not been successful.

Then he had this experience: despite the pain,
His soul was gladdened, and all the more so;
It was as if the contradiction drew him upwards.

It is not right that the soul should consume itself,
When it knows that God is near.
Thou hast heard about the deceiving devil.

If thou carriest the Lord in thy heart —
Because thou hast been faithful to Him throughout the years —
Truth smiles through the burden of life.

LXXV

One says that this or that will give thee joy;
There is nothing to object to in this.
However: the joy that keeps watch in thy heart
Is greater still; so be content with it.

Blessèd be the joy that the Lord
Has placed in thee from the beginning.
It is the foundation of existence and of the spirit —
Happy the man who cherishes his peace in it.

LXXVI

Be not surprised that, when the devil threatens,
An angel smiles in order to console thy heart;
Pure Being is more profound than evil's misery.

Even in blasphemy there is God's love —
Thus said a sage, and what he meant was that
It is impossible for satan to elude God.

LXXVII

One knows not whether the world is a vale of tears,
In which some scattered joys are to be found —
Or is made of pleasures without number,
In which all sufferings vanish like the wind.

It is immaterial where the truth lies —
The world and life are what thou art.

LXXVIII

The good, it has been said, is an absolute;
And so the pain of punishment is merciless.
But this overlooks that compassion pertains to the good,
And that no soul can be totally bad.

"With what measure ye mete, it shall be measured unto you again" —
"Let him who is without sin cast the first stone."
Nevertheless: the judge must represent the law;
He cannot forgive the wicked man's deeds.

"First be reconciled, then offer thy gift."
Does this mean thou shouldst abstain from judging,
And no longer see what is good or bad?
Thou mayest surely discern, but thou mayest not hate.

Think of the bliss of Heaven's meadows —
Bitterness does not exist in Paradise.

LXXIX

Are there flames that blaze eternally?
One had to threaten with hellfire
Because evil people exist: it had to be described
As an absolute and not be minimized —
For the weal of the wicked and the protection of the good.

God's rods strike according to His will.

LXXX

The Heavens are segments — from rim to center —
And each is divided into levels.
Religions are different worlds,
But they have similar prayers, similar invocations:
Peoples who are united in the selfsame love —

For they all live by the Great One.

LXXXI

There is no mass without energy;
How could one question this?
There can be no existence without power —
Without the luminous waves of the creative will.

Physical proof is doubtful
When it distorts the nature of existence —
The metaphysical axiom suffices.

LXXXII

Number is without limit, it grows and swells;
Such is the world — who can count all things?
The fraction, which endlessly divides the One —
This is the way that sages have chosen.

The way inward: rejoice within this space,
Which frees and makes thee infinite.
The outer world is narrow, it wants to afflict thee.
If thou livest toward the inward, thou hast awoken —

Awoken in the heart's space, which is God's alone.

LXXXIII

Gross manifestation in the outward, subtle manifestation in the inward:
Matter and psyche; corporeal forms
Throughout the universe; then powers of the soul,
Which are suprasensory. Cosmic norms.

The Last Judgment: everywhere the corporeal
Is absorbed into the subtle —
The world passes. But it returns later,
As if newly created from a rainbow.

LXXXIV

The earth is spoiled and poisoned —
It is like lead, black and heavy;
It can never again be pure or renewed,
Except by dissolution from Above.

You may know the essentials about the future,
But never attempt to see the details clearly,
For they belong to God. In His Hands
Lies everything. He alone has to build the world.

LXXXV

In earthly existence, thou canst not avoid
Suffering from the poison of evil thorns.
The serpent was already there in Adam's time —
The evil one thus dwells in every soul.

Beware that in his bitter jealousy
He does not rob thee of thy faith in God;
Holy indifference is always the best remedy —
When thou listenest not, the enemy cannot enter.

LXXXVI

The scales of God thou canst not understand;
Small may be the reasons for salvation,
Small those for damnation. Great may be
Heaven's indulgence — a ray from an aspect
Of the universe. According to the possibilities of destiny,
A grace may take effect which pardons beyond measure.

LXXXVII

Prose is fresh, unfettered thinking;
Poetry seeks to give us speech in beauty.
Epic poetry is symbolism — who will kill the dragon;
Lyrical poetry is the nostalgic song of Krishna's flute.

Prose is thinking, but prosody
Thinks with music: it is the transition
From walking to dancing; it is an overflowing —
It transmutes form into drunken melody.

LXXXVIII

The hands of man manifest his heart;
Whence the *mudrā* of the priest: a power of blessing
That links the earthly to the heavenly;
Or a ray of wrath, sent by God.

An instrument may prolong the priestly hand:
Such as the *dorje* and the *vajra* which, combined with a *mudrā*,
Bestow the lama's blessing on the soul.
And the prayer-wheel that is turned by the pious —

The blessing is blown over the whole world.

LXXXIX

South-east Asia — celestial dances
That came from India, mostly from the Ramayana;
Beautiful dancers: little girls,
Charming children — but their art is difficult.

Temple dances: golden images of the gods —
With gamelan and ancient Hindu melodies;
Static dance, almost motionless, but enraptured —

Like the stars that circle the heavens.

XC

Build the temple, not the Tower of Babel;
The fall of the Titans — many fables confirm this.
"Noblesse oblige" — I must not remain silent:
If thou wilt build something, then build thy soul.

What animals build is not a new creation;
Only *homo faber* can freely invent.
As the image of God, he seeks to proclaim anew
The world, himself and God.

XCI

Man needs canonical prayer —
God wills that we think of Him in a rhythm;
Certainly, we can go freely to the Most High —
Nevertheless, God wills to guide the steps of the people.

For if the individual wishes to enjoy the Lord,
There must be a framework for all:
The Lord's Prayer and the *Fātiha* —
And long before these, the *Shemā*.

If there were not divine bread from which to live —
The possibility of wine would not exist.

XCII

The tribes of the tropical forest have religions,
But they believe in witchcraft and are degenerate.
Nevertheless, quite often, even in these dark places,
One finds words of true wisdom
That could teach any skeptic.
So, whoever's child the spirit may be, one must honor him.

XCIII

Why lovest thou, O soul, from time to time,
The songs of warlike Cossack horsemen?
Doubtless because in what is stormy, strong and wild,
Nobility also resounds — a contradictory image;
Just as, on blood-stained battlefields,
Life and death go hand in hand.

XCIV

Why wast thou moved by gypsy violins,
Songs that penetrated deeply into thy soul —
Why is love woven into thy heart?

In every longing throbs an urge to the Above.

XCV

Sun, gold, lion, honey,
Pheasant, sunflower, bee —
And the corresponding human types,
It is as if the sun shone through their faces.

Then moon, silver and snow:
A glowing, but softened and subdued;
A family of mild things, like moonlight —
And like the water-lily, and the lily.

Purusha and *Prakriti* — signs of God,
Which penetrate through creation a thousandfold.

XCVI

"Burn what thou hast adored,
Adore what thou hast burnt":
Thus spake a preacher to a king —
A heathen, who understood nothing of faith.
The king — from a Germanic tribe — became a Christian:
For his own sake, and not in defiance of his ancestors.
Many things happen in this world —
But never will the noble man deny what he is.

XCVII

Metaphysics speaks of final things
Which transcend worldly phenomena;
Cosmology speaks of the latter:
It provides answers to questions about existence.
Mysticism is the science of the soul
On its path to the Sovereign Good;
Psychology treats of the fabric
Of the earthly soul — and also of nobility.

What does the theologian know? Spiritual realities —
But seen from the angle of a particular faith:
The Divine Being, then His holy Will —
So that man may fulfill his life's duty.
Literalism must be in the workings of Scripture,
Otherwise nothing of the message would remain.

XCVIII

Metaphysics, said a Jesuit,
Is a wonderful thing.
But it is not necessary for salvation.
See to it, that thy soul do what is right.

He was right, but only for himself;
Not for the philosopher — not for me.
I do not offer empty words —
Metaphysics is a way to salvation.

I quarrel not and I let others be —
Nowhere can anything better than Truth be found.
Nothing can rejoice the spirit more than this:
The highest Truth is the Being of God.

XCIX

Why repeat things endlessly?
We do not do this; consider a mountain in the country:
Its many different aspects are without number —
Yet it is one, and thou walkest round its rim.

A single word branches out, it becomes finer —
In a thousand words, the meaning is but one.
Thou canst see the same thing in the religions:
The true wishes to dwell in different places.

C

Each poem has its own argument—
It seeks not to contest with others.
See how the independent thoughts
Finally interweave into one meaning.

No one composed a single saying —
Each truth thought itself.

CI

In the Face of God, I seek to know nothing —
For what I should know, God knows it best.
The Most High's Wisdom contains the essence of things,
It encompasses the world, from east to west —
From the first day to the last hour.

The "I" is like the moon, now big, now small;
The sun remains true to itself — God is pure Being.

In the Face of God, I can lack nothing —
So let joy delight in Joy.

CII

What is it that makes man miserable?
Matter and worldliness, not "woman and gold,"
As a yogi said, because he saw
Only temptation. — If destiny favors thee,
It can bring thee the best wife;
And without money, no one can live.

Matter is impurity and brings suffering;
Worldliness is not mandatory — one can abstain from it.

CIII

When passion is combined with profundity,
Or joy of life with melancholy —
See how enchanting is the rapture's melody,
Because it is based on the profound mystery of existence.

In the dance of life's *Māyā* , may there shine
Primordial sounds that reach unto the Most High.

CIV

The ancient East is based on Truth —
But it comprises errors that cause dismay.
The modern West is erroneous in itself —
But nevertheless it has its good sides.

Whence comes the misery of history?
It is not merely the to-and-fro of time;
Nor the caprice of distant gods —
It is the pettiness of the majority of men.

CV

Strength of will is not aggressiveness; and likewise
The pride of the noble man does not mean that he is puffed-up;
The fool confuses the two, because he cannot
Understand the magnanimity of superior men.

He whose small "I" keeps him prisoner,
Does not understand the world of the free man.

CVI

One of the things that makes us happiest
Is to give happiness to others. Who can
Enjoy happiness without sharing it?
Our friends should experience the peace of one's soul.

The sun shines and the heavens give rain —
Like this shouldst thou also give of the riches of thy heart.

CVII

Love is not mere sentimental play,
It is also the wish to benefit the other soul;
Whoever truly and selflessly loves someone,
Will protect that person's God-consecrated heart.

Taking and giving: during life —
But with a view to immortality.

CVIII

If thou saw'st the dance of hips and breasts,
The face as if 'twere sunken in deep sleep,
As if she nothing knew of earthly life —
If thou saw'st Leila, how her body sways,

As if about to soar to the world of light,
She would lift up thy soul to Heaven.
Thou wouldst think: if only my heart could learn to dance —
In God's nearness and far from earth.

CIX

Whom God unites, let no man put asunder,
Thus it is said. But whom does God unite?
Not always what seems opportune to parents —
Not a he and a she who cannot love each other.

Blessing cannot be in pious lies;
It is found deep in the nature of things.

CX

Love, it is said, lasts only for a time —
But within itself love carries eternity;
And in this deep indwelling lies
The possibility that love will conquer time.

CXI

"Father, forgive the sinners, for they know not
What they do." Most surely, but this does not mean
That God will erase every debt,
And that the wicked will never have to expiate.

For there is guilt and guilt: one comes
From an evil heart, but the other depends
On dogmas. Wickedness will be condemned;
But God forgives the one in whom He finds truth.

CXII

The hereafter is not worldly, people say,
And rightly so — and consequently it is pure emptiness;
Yes and no. One should not misunderstand:
There is nothing that the Highest Power lacks.

Let not good news disturb your seriousness:
God always gives more than what His word has promised.
The Good wishes that its radiation spread.

CXIII

The Arabs told me: slowness
Comes from the All-Merciful; haste comes from the devil.
Certitude is the way of the Most High —
The light of Truth. Doubt comes from the evil one.

Prudenter agas, finem respice;
People also say, "slow but sure"
And "make haste slowly" — *festina lente.*
In all your actions, keep the end in view!

CXIV

Everywhere there is the risk of misusing what is good:
Good becomes a vice when it is exaggerated
Or wrongly applied. Moderation is a virtue,
Importuning is not. Love your neighbor.

When ye give alms, take care:
"Let not the left hand see what the right is doing."

CXV

The Master, they say, is a superman;
How can I help it if many people
Love darkness, or that I must shine?
I am not responsible for today's accursed world.

May God take pity on our poor world —
The Master too belongs to the world of the poor.

CXVI

Self-respect is natural in the noble man,
But self-contempt is too, in another sense:
One values for itself whatever comes from the Good;
One does not wish that evil power should triumph.

For thou art nothing before God. But His seal
Is upon thee; thou art the God-consecrated mirror.

CXVII

I know, I will, I can, I do —
This is the path to highest peace.
I do what my will can;
I will what my mind has been able to know:
The sacred meaning of earthly life.
I know and will that which I am.

For: "I am small, my heart is pure" —
My very being dwells in God's Will.

CXVIII

What distinguishes a butterfly
From a man? The "I" of the insect
Is divided into a thousand individuals,
Whereas with us, the thousandfold possibility
Dwells within one single ego —

May God deliver the totality of our soul.

CXIX

Of what does the "I" consist? Firstly, of the impulses
That remain in the soul from long ago;
Of character traits from our parents
That have steered the "I" along many paths;
Then of the colorful dance of experience —
Of things that show the soul's intention;
And finally of Heaven's "yes" and grace,
Which help us ascend on the path of destiny.

To be cured of all bad accretions,
To become what we have always been in our archetype:
In the creative Will that made man
As a likeness, and brought him the light of salvation.

The "I" is a mixture of nothing and everything —
A spark which is finally extinguished in God.

CXX

As sparks flash forth in the cold night
And then expire, but are preserved
In the fire's substance — so we are cast
Into existence. Thus did the Lord conceive us —

He radiated His Being into the naught of the other;
Being wishes to rest in Selfhood — but also to move outwards.

CXXI

Let not thyself be troubled by the phantoms
Brought thee by thy soul in order to delude thee —
Clouds of fog cannot endure;
Let them dissolve before the Spirit's walls.
The tempter may well threaten us with ruses;
The Light keeps watch — the delusion is gone.

There is within us a slight contradiction
That comes from the fact that the world is transient;
And even the best that destiny bestows
Is in many respects insufficient —
Compared with the Absolute Good.
"It is ever well with the believer" —

For God looks now into thy soul.
The believer wills to be now, not later.

CXXII

I am here, where I am. I could be
Elsewhere: in a city on the Rhine,
Or by the sea, on a mountain top;
Or in other places that I see in my soul —

But I am here. Both a naught and an all —
A nowhere, and a here in the kingdom of Heaven.

CXXIII

Neti, neti — "not this, not this" — why cannot
The Highest Divinity be encompassed
In words? Because the True dwells nowhere —
And yet is tangible everywhere.

Just as ether permeates all space
And is contained in every substance,
So is *Ananda* — God's beatitude —
The luminous substance, on which the universe is based.

In the structure of the universe, some points are wounds;
But Pure Being is its luminous essence.

CXXIV

Where wilt thou dwell in eternity?
In Primordial Being, which bestows on thee new being —
In God, when everything has merged in Him.
We no longer have any desire outside of God.

Thou canst not penetrate into the fullness of God —
Into Him, Who is self-subsistent.
Yet it is His Will to penetrate into us —

Mahāpralaya, apocatástasis.

CXXV

Two doors has the earthly life of man:
Birth and death, and each of them is suffering.
In life itself there are sufferings and joys —
In the hereafter God weaves only one of these.

Different things lie in the word "eternity";
May the Lord grant that ye know the enigma:
The final word is beatitude —

Because beatitude is the essence of the Most High.

CXXVI

The *Kalki-Avatāra*, it is written,
Will soon come at the end of this yuga —
Riding on a white horse;
At his side will be all the noble, pious men
Who ever fought for the victory of Truth.

CXXVII

Om namo sarva Tathāgata Om —
Salutation to all the saints of this world!
May the illusory world finally become
The country of the Spirit and of true Peace!

For "Thy kingdom come" — and Thy will be done,
In this earthly vale as in Heaven's heights.

CXXVIII

Vairāgya — equanimity and serenity,
I longed for grace;
I did not find that joy, it was too far —
But blessing came to me, and became my own self.

CXXIX

An enigma of destiny is man's activity:
Its fruits follow in its tracks.
The question is whether the soul is made beautiful,
Or whether it foolishly destroys itself.

So hold fast to what makes holy,
And flee from what drags down.
The best act is the one that mentions the Lord,
And sees His presence in the heart.

CXXX

On doomsday, it is said, men tremble,
Frightened to death; God's thunder speaks.
But not the one who let the Most High dwell in him —
For God in our heart trembles not.

CXXXI

Serenity and Certitude — and likewise:
Resignation and trust. Ye should know
That this is the path through life's dream;
So be trusting, and walk on both feet.

It is said that the sage is always happy —
One should overcome the vacillations of the soul
And, already here below, one should find
In the earthly play of things, what one will find in God.

CXXXII

In old age, one does not have much choice;
One always wonders: is this the last time?
One has not, as in youth, before oneself
A space that is as rich as the world in its dream.

How is it, when the soul feels no age
Because, outside of time, it always stood
In the eternal Now that aims toward the Heights?

Thou surely foundest what others did not find —
Thou didst not understand what did not understand thee,
And thou wast with God in thy best hours.

CXXXIII

Thou livest in this world, not in the next;
Thou think'st that there thou wouldst be happy.
Earthly soul, be still: here as well as there
God is the Sovereign Good — and He alone.

We are in this world in order to manifest
The Word of Truth and the circle of our way.
Say not we know not this or that —
As long as we know that God knows it.

Songs without Names

Second Collection

Each poem has its own argument —
It seeks not to contest with others.
See how the independent thoughts
Finally interweave into one meaning.

No one composed a single saying —
Each truth thought itself.

Songs without Names

Second Collection

I

In this world, the pious man carries God's grace;
In the next world, God's grace carries the pious man.
In this world, man must earn
What he receives.
                    Heaven says: welcome.

II

Be careful before ye reject faith;
Ask not a priori how and when.
Take note that without the support of faith,
Earthly humanity cannot endure.

This proves that in the religions
Dwell the deepest elements of Truth;
God did not bring the world a false Word,
For man is made for Truth.

Mother faith and Mother earth —
The Good Shepherd, and salvation's flock.

III

God's Word is like the globe of the earth:
We are made for the earth; for us it is a protection.
Starry space is an icy night;
So too is the deadly poison of doubt — one wants to flee,
To find a homeland, to go far away —
To find oneself, but one knows not where.

God has chosen the earth for us;
We were not born on Jupiter.
Mother faith and Mother earth —
They remove from the soul the pain of fear.

IV

Ye ask: can religion be a homeland?
I give the answer: yes and no;
Yes, because faith is a form of Truth;
But absolutely true is the pure Spirit alone.

Religion in its devotional form
Humanizes God and admits only will,
Sentiment and worship; it underestimates
Values that are clad in foreign forms.

Each faith offers eternal reward —
For each is a form of the One Religion.

V

The Creator and Savior is Being;
In Beyond-Being is All-Possibility;
God brings possibilities — in accordance with
Their inherent tendencies — into the wide world of existence.

Wisdom is a thirst to know, but also a renunciation —
Know what is important; and do not ask too much.

VI

Angustia — fear of life: this is a madness
Hatched by our ailing times;
There was no fear of existence in times of faith,
Which strongly protected souls

And made them happy. With the wound of doubt
Our souls and our world collapse.

VII

Just as, with warmth, ice becomes water,
So the body becomes dance and words become music.
The solid form that shapes our everyday life
Melts away and returns to its Substance.

Likewise the heart before God, in the sun of the Spirit:
The solid individuality returns to Bliss.

VIII

A noble man is he who thinks objectively,
And never lets bitterness arise within him —
Who understands, without vain stubbornness,
How human riddles have a meaning.

A noble man accepts what God has destined:
What must be, cannot but be — take heed,
Become not bitter; if feelings of hatred
Well up within thy soul, thou art thyself the illusion.

And then it is superfluous to dispute —
Only the fight against thy specter has meaning.

IX

There are so many people who love to listen
To the noise of disguised praise of themselves,
And think that they are good and noble —
And strew false nobility into the air.

Nobility is not the noise of self-love;
The noble man abhors narcissistic tendencies;
He looks serenely on the nature of things —
He leaves it to others to read the mystery of his person.

The noble man — he stands firmly before God;
Not so the hypocrite, who gambles himself away —
He should walk before God in sackcloth and ashes.

X

The devil contrives that even pious people
Do not want to know what the devil is;
They seek to explain in a natural way
What, in reality, are the ruses of the evil one.
This confuses things in their mind:
They see the defects, but not satan's noose.

When thy soul walks on the path to the Most High,
Then know that the devil is watching for thee.

XI

Self-assurance is a fragile thing.
Thou hast certitude, because there is Truth —
But this does not prove thou art like unto it;
Be happy, if God forgives thee thy humanity.

XII

The world is crooked, but stand thou upright before God;
He will not judge thee for the sins of others.
Thou bearest responsibility only for thine own deeds —
Before God thou canst destroy only thine own illusions.

It may well grieve thee that the world is askew —
But not too much; thou canst always love God.

XIII

The Lord is completely free — it has been said —
To do what He wishes: to place the wicked
In paradise, without any reason,
And the righteous in the fire of hell.

This is pious stupidity. God's Will is
Not human will, it is the ray of Truth —
It is pure Justice.
Absurdity is not, for God, an object of choice.

The freedom of God: the Infinite,
In Pure Being, is not like the finite.

XIV

Have you seen how the soap bubble
In delicate, shimmering colors rises and falls,
Floats upward, then is lost in the grass
And is no more — so it is with the world

And with life. But not with the heart
That has seen God. Just as in a holy shrine
The consecrated candles stand motionless in devotion
Before God — so shall thy heart be also.

XV

My first homeland was the Germanic environment,
A world of poetry; it was taken from me,
One wanted to re-educate me and destroy me —
I would gladly have swum back across the Rhine.
In an alien land, in the midst of post-war psychosis,
Suffering came — "That's where my sadness began."

But then Vedanta came into my life:
Metaphysics, cogently expounded;
The language was French. The second homeland
For me was Wisdom and the whole world;
And all the sadness of my youth was worthwhile —
For the homeland is where Truth dwells.

XVI

Inspiration comes — the writing is easy;
Heavy is the burden of the Whole; easy is what has been given —
Heavy is the responsibility. I would like to keep silent —
God knows best; and so I receive even more.

Thou askest me, O reader, who the writer is;
I know not; and may God pardon me.

XVII

The greatest miracle that the angels work
Is that their activity can give life to the naught —
And so arises: first the dream of the universe,
And then — it cannot be otherwise —the foam of evil.

It must be so: because the existence of this world
Coincides with its play of shadows;
Where there is light, there must also be darkness;
Pure Light — it shines in God alone.

XVIII

The wheel of time turns. All things must move,
Says Heraclitus. The wise man does not see anything
Without seeing through it to its kernel.

Thus for him, the flow of things stands still
In the midst of its movement, which no man
Can escape, even if he wishes otherwise.

A contradiction? — nay, a true showing
Of timeless Being in all earthly things.

XIX

The Virgin: "clothed with the sun alone,"
The Scriptures say. What might the sun be?
The golden light that comes from on high,
Illuminating her limbs, delicate and fine.

The Virgin is the Truth unveiled,
Beautiful as love and pure as snow —
The sun is the Spirit that unveils her
And so transforms water into wine.

XX

A man recited ceaselessly his prayer —
And finally became one with his Word.
The Word became one with him, who stood
Timelessly before his God, and became a sacred place

Filled with God's Presence. If thou becomest a star —
The star is thine, a gift bestowed by the Lord.

XXI

Is it not strange how the smallest of things
Can give us delight, even in our later years,
When we are wise and full of experience —
And more detached than ever before.

This is because we never outlive the child within us,
And rightly so, for it bears witness to Heaven.
What is great can shimmer through what is small,
For God ceaselessly shows us His Goodness.

Life brings us much, the path is long —
God appreciates in us simple gratitude.

XXII

I do not criticize the penitent or the ascetic;
Far from it. Nevertheless,
Their special vocation is not a duty
For everyone, before the Face of God.

Men's capacities differ,
And so do the starting-points of their spiritual paths.
Whatever saves our soul can never be wrong;
Gnosis is not for everyone.

What is sin against the Holy Ghost?
Denial of a truth that one knows,
Or should know, if one were honest.
Cursèd is he who separates himself from the True.

XXIII

"Sensible consolations," says theology
With a frown. That something that pleases God
May be found in the agreeable —
This will never enter the heads of the teachers of asceticism.

In a word: man must walk on both feet:
One step says no, the other step says yes.
Of course, one can stress either the yes or the no —
The essential is where one sees the Most High.

XXIV

Uninterrupted by the wheel of time,
Always in the turmoil of daily cares —
It seems as if one could lose one's mind;
No wonder people are constantly fleeing:

Not only from things, but also from themselves —
The life of the average man is flight.
Consciousness of Truth is the only rock;
God, it is said, has cursed all the rest.

But not what is linked with one's sense of God,
And, indirectly, guides the soul's steps.

XXV

Hair-splitting about the nature of God
Has been a danger from earliest times.
But when the wise man thinks,
He accepts whatever God gives him.

XXVI

As a child, I once imagined I was in
A dark, cold forest, and before me in the distance,
I saw a Christmas tree,
And above it a sweet choir of angels;

I drew near this golden warmth
Of pine boughs, richly hung with ornaments
And red candles — and I thought to myself:
It is thus that, one day, I would like to enter Paradise.

XXVII

They built for me a beautiful wooden house
In a forest where deer live —
And spiritual friends dwell all around;
A few Indian tents are pitched nearby.

It is a little earthly paradise,
Made so that, undisturbed, one may strive upwards,
Towards the archetype, about which the soul knows full well.

XXIX

I-consciousness is a two-edged sword;
A restriction, but also something precious:
A key, not to thinking, but to being;
Be what thou thinkest, when thou art alone with God.

XXX

Man arose from God's creative power;
But later, man created his own image.

Yet we are extinguished in holy repentance —
In God-remembrance, He creates us anew.

XXXI

Al-Hallāj said that he was God — who knows
Why he said it. — Abu Yazīd said:
"Glory be to me." Love-mysticism
May express itself as if in drunkenness or dream —

The gnostic will not walk on ice;
He too drinks wine — but never becomes drunk.

XXXII

Ask not the question: what is going to happen?
Let things come to thee as they come.
Be at peace in the Now
That belongs to God; thy faith will reward thee.

If thy thoughts turn to the Most High,
He is with thee; and whatever lies before thee,
In this world and the next, is in His Hands.

XXXIII

People do what wears out their spirit,
Then run to the doctor, who is supposed to heal them;
It is indifferent to him that their soul is dying —
The remedy is to rush towards the naught.

Do what is reasonable; seek for help from the Lord;
Then ye will be at peace and will act with joy.

XXXIV

Securitas — people are obsessed with the illusion
That a golden security could exist on earth;
An absolute protection against the moods of destiny,
As if the vale of tears could become Heaven.

Seek for security where it exists —
In the Sovereign Good, that never fades.

XXXV

In the *krita-yuga*, space was so wide,
That it could bring time to a standstill;
In the *kali-yuga*, the world rushes ceaselessly —
More and more, our space becomes time.

The turmoil of time, brethren, ye must resist —
There is no haste in the land of Wisdom.

XXXVI

"Existentialism" is a thinking
That no longer wishes to think; this means the destruction
Of the true thinking that constitutes man.
The existentialist fanatics
Dislocate their brains for nothing — it is only a case of
Self-delusion and self-promotion.

For to think truly means: recollection.
Let the fools spin their foolishness.

XXXVII

A villain hates thee — and yet
Thou shouldst not hate him; what then mayst thou feel?
Thou shouldst see him as he is, no more, no less;
Thou shouldst not rage in anger.

For he is a possibility that one must
Acknowledge. Perhaps he can be helped
By the lofty mind with which one discriminates;

Perhaps not: if poison is at the bottom of his feelings,
This condemns him. Man becomes what he wills.

XXXVIII

Many people, both male and female,
Wish to find a perfect love; O longing, be at peace.
There is indeed a partner, for the world is wide —
But the question is whether thy destiny wills it.

It may be that, in your world,
Ye lack this or that — when in fact only the Sovereign Good
Is the solace and crowning of our wanderings —

The Lord, in Whom love's being is rooted.

XXXIX

Al-Qutb — the Pole, it is called in Sufism;
He is the tall lighthouse of his time:
He teaches about all things, near and far —
About Being, life, death and eternity.

He teaches not only how to think — but also how to be,
Deep within one's heart; for to understand means to become.
Truth and beauty — their concordance is everything;
There is nothing better on earth.

XL

The most beautiful thing that the senses, or the soul,
Can experience here and now on earth
Lasts but a moment — yet it is an image
Of the eternal — of what thou shouldst become.

It is not what thou in worldliness has kindled,
But what has penetrated to thy inmost depth —
And what thou findest in the Truth of the Most High —

It is what the angels of Love sang before time began.

XLI

Man is the likeness of God:
Man and woman; so it is written.
That the body is sin, was added later —
The opposition has been pushed too far.

The body's worship is either fasting or dancing;
King David teaches both.
When fasting, one regrets the deceit of the flesh;
In dancing, one honors the image of God.

XLII

Faith is the spiritual strength
Which, from the center, creates all good;
Patience is the disposition of the soul
That rests in the present, in the now.

Faith, accompanied by patience: this is the equilibrium
That promises God's blessing for salvation —
O golden Center, which no longer questions;
O luminous Now, which contains all.

The earthly world flows back into thy heart;
Thy whole life is but a blessèd moment.

XLIII

Painters of the Far East love clouds of mist —
Why so? Because all existence is mysterious;
Yang, yin: between the two poles, a to-and-fro,
A veiling and unveiling: the play
That produces this world and also our thoughts.

Dance has the same double meaning:
The veils that conceal and reveal,
Just as the mist rises and flees —

The Tao — Path of the Marvelous One.

XLIV

In God-remembrance remain far from the world —
For God's rule over it is not thy concern.
Providence watches over earthly din —
But remain thou with the Most High: watch and pray.

Even without thee, the world-wheel continues to turn.
Look toward the solace that removed thy sorrow from thee;
The world may be dark — but the Word is bright;

The Divine Word, that came into thy heart.

XLV

So many things has thine active mind thought —
And thou hast written them down, saying well nigh everything;
But when thou meetest God, this multiplicity
Becomes transformed into the beatitude of one same sound —

Just as in a song, a single note
Sings of the golden overflowing of the soul.

XLVI

What I think and what I am,
I should not keep begrudgingly within me;
For my existence has a meaning for others —
And the secret powers of the Spirit belong to God.

XLVII

God doeth what He wills, and wills what comes to pass
By His Activity — there is no difference;
For God's Spirit is not a magic wand;
Whatever be His Will — He is the Good.

What we distinguish as good and evil
Is what we experience — what we love or avoid;
God wills not evil as such, nay —
He permits only what, inevitably, is the shadow of the Good.

Infinity, All-Possibility — the wheel
That reason can understand only with difficulty.

XLVIII

We distinguish between two kinds of ugliness:
One can be attractive and noble,
And bears witness to the weaknesses and moods of nature;
The other is obnoxious and mean,
And a denial of what is noble;
We avoid it, as we avoid evil.

We hate no one; our heart stays pure
On this ever-changing earthly meadow.
Not that feelings should crown what is false —
We love beauty, but not everything beautiful.

A particular kind of beauty is
The beauty of old age, which ye must appreciate.

XLIX

Whether or not one may say something ugly?
The answer is partly yes and partly no —
Certainly, the means should not be ugly;
It is better to avoid bad speech.

Tribute to this world we have to pay:
And what is of use, one may express.

L

Faqīr, "one who is poor," is the dervish-brother —
Not only poor "for God," but also poor "in God";
For to the earthly creature, Being seems poor —
To consecrate oneself to God means the death of the soul.

And yet we know that all this is but appearance —
Being is ever rich and limitless.
Truly to grasp this is pure faith —
Be happy with the Divine Nature.

What is the stage that can no longer err?
When poverty, through wisdom, becomes wealth.

LI

It is said that ye should hold firmly onto forms;
For it is they that shape the fabric of the soul.
But when the Essential Content has accepted thee,
This will benefit thee more than mere prescriptions.

LII

Thou goest from one dwelling-place to another,
And suddenly thou no longer feelest at home;
Everything seems strange to thee. Fear not —
In God-remembrance is a secure refuge.

Estrangement disappears; the alarm
Was illusion. In God thou shalt discover thyself anew.

LIII

Prayer — firstly it is commanded;
And then: the soul has dire need of it.
It is not a case of merely doing what pleases thee —
The one who prays brings blessing to the world.

Thy prayer must show a pure intention —
Otherwise it cannot rise to God's heights.

LIV

Livest thou in space? This must be somewhere;
And in time? This must be some time;
Thou canst not escape these particularities —
Thine is what destiny can give.

Tell thyself, what the will of God ordains for thee
Is noble existence — is Being itself.

LV

It is strange that in brave peoples'
Zest for life there is a kind of greatness:
Skamarinskaya — when the god of life,
Or the god of war, sways back and forward in the dance.

What appeals to thee stems from the archetype —
In every drop of water dreams the sea.

LVI

Despise not what artists of this world
Offer, when the work is a sign
Of cosmic reality, coming from Above —
A becoming-visible that flows out of light.

The man may be the instrument, quite unconsciously,
Of something based on the highest values.

LVII

Reason, sentiment, imagination and memory:
They are, in the ego, the legacy of the pure Spirit —
North, South, East, West. These are the faculties
That lead soul and body through earthly life.

They are contained within the Self of the Creator,
They are, in the world, the driving forces:
Wisdom, love, creative power, and then
Peace; blessèd the soul that has attained it.

LVIII

Metaphysics — what is one supposed to know?
Discernment between Beyond-Being,
Being and Existence; then the difference
Between world and soul; between appearance
And reality; and their connecting link,
Māyā, which can be both.

The Intellect looks at the "I" and is not blind.
It sees that all around are other souls,
Who also call themselves "I" —
How can one separate the "thou" from an "I"?
This is the limitless play of *Māyā* —
Ātmā is unique, but multiple is the world.

On the one hand, the Good wishes to overflow,
On the other hand: it wishes to enjoy its deep Self.

LIX

Mā shā'a 'Llāh — Allāh karīm —
So say the Moslems.
"What God wished, has happened."
We must accept it from Him.

Yet "God is benevolent" — this must
Be added, and should delight us;
For, in all situations, God will
Watch over us, be we near or far.

LX

There is a river called the soul —
Why dost thou enter into it?
O spirit, thou canst be
Much happier on the bank.

Look at the tree that timeless stands
On the edge of this stream:
The river rushes on, it knows not whither —
The tree stands firmly on the land.

LXI

Depth of spirit — this is accompanied
By beauty of soul; but, conversely,
A beautiful psyche can be independent
Of spirituality, as experience shows.
By its charm, youth's magic can illumine
Life's earthbound nature;
But these are values that do not reach the truly inward —
They are merely the play of *Māyā* with the outward.

In the beautiful, the sacred is honored —
A vain person is unworthy of beauty.

Splendor of the Truth — this was Plato's oath.

LXII

Remembrance of God — thinking of the One;
Why is the One so powerful?
Oneness seems little when thou countest;
The world is rich and great and multiform —

But it has not the quality of simplicity.
Ambiguity is imperfection;
The world is full of fissures, contradictions —
Too many cooks are in its kitchen.

Look at the circle or the sphere: it is wonderful
To be so homogeneous and so entirely oneself.

LXIII

See'st thou the rock in the middle of the ocean?
See'st thou how the waves roar around it?
Or in mild weather, how they
Lovingly caress the hard stone;

The stone — the Spirit, that stands in Truth.
Strong is the heart, though it contains sweetness too;
Surrounded by life's spring breeze and storm —

The heart, that carries God's love and message.

LXIV

What makes thee completely happy? Thy "yes" to God;
This comes first in the spiritual life.
But thou art in the world, thou art not alone;
So the second happiness of the heart is giving.

The giving of what thy believing "yes"
Has given thee; the giving of what thy heart's depth has seen.

LXV

A winter fairy tale. Snow covers the land —
The fairy queen comes in her silver sleigh;
You hear the tiny bells and see the whirlwind dance ——
Snowflakes, falling from heavy branches.

Snow — like eternity's shroud,
Extinguishing all vain differences —
As if Pure Being had laid Itself
On this and that — as if the world would die,

Or else renew itself in the sphere
Of archetypes, where there is no change.

LXVI

Didst thou see the morning sun on the snow,
How it gilds what is shining like silver?
Thus it is, when something of God's consolation
Shimmers through the cool forms of His Truth.

What seemed like a distant purity, far from thee,
Comes to meet thee, like a greeting from the Lord.

LXVII

Thou findest world-negation and God-affirmation
In the words: *lā ilāha illa 'Llāh.*
Then follows a "yes" for God's act of creation,
In the words: *Muhammadun Rasūlu 'Llāh.*

Therein lies everything: our world is appearance,
For God alone is Pure Reality;
But the world is a ray from God's Being.

LXVIII

Fata Morgana — is it not an illusion?
The real oasis is far off — thine eye
Sees only air. Nevertheless, remember:
A rose manifests itself through its fragrance.

Thus it is with everything good in the world:
What one deems to be only earthly, comes from God.

LXIX

The *bhakta* loves, but not the *jñāni* —
So many think, and are stubborn
In their logic: for, after all, it is without feeling
That one counts that one and one are two.

But different is what I have seen in my heart —
The True, that seizes my whole self;
The heart wishes to become what the brain understands —
Whoever sees *Ātmā* is close to love.

One can think of many things without loving —
But not of That which impels us to love.
To love God means: in Him is our happiness —
Thinking of *Ātmā*, the heart becomes music.

LXX

Killing is impossible for the *brahmana*;
For the *kshatriya*, killing is a holy duty;
The *brahmana* agrees with this,
But the warrior's work does not befit him.

The *brahmana* is there to clear the way
To the Divine. The *kshatriya* must look to the
People's well-being and to his ancestors' heritage;
He must — as his *dharma* demands — be noble,
And attend to the protection of spiritual treasures.
Brahma is real, and the world is appearance.

The *brahmana* — he is the bridge-builder;
The *kshatriya* — his concern is only the wall.
The sanctuary, protected in a secure shrine.

LXXI

The saint, the sage, the hero and
The martyr; each has his particular radiance,
And is a consolation for this poor world.

The saint: he is the image of virtue;
From the sage radiates the Truth, that delivers;
The hero is our sword and our shield;
The martyr bears the suffering of all men.

Thus each, with his particular gift, shines
Into this vale of tears; may God grant
That every man may have in him something of each one.

LXXII

You ask what may the hero mean for us —
Which heavenly archetype could produce him.
Archangel Michael, with his sword —
Have you never heard of his power?

And God's wrath — it was already there;
For God's "no" must accompany God's "yes."
You ask: was God not first pure mildness?
The possibility of wrath was also part of the picture.

The martyr — what is the meaning of his sacrifice?
The Creator projected Himself into His creation.
He shone, so to speak, into the naught —
He willed to be other than Himself.

LXXIII

The saint can work miracles. How
Can this be? Our reasoning is silent.
God wills to reveal His power;
The saint is the instrument that shows it.

LXXIV

At the end of all time and all worlds,
Thou wilt return, O man, to the Divine;
There thou hast already been, and hast waited for thyself;
All that is belovèd is in this happiness.

Nothing can enter into the realm of the Most High —
Absolute plenitude is without change.
Thou canst not bring the Lord thy poverty —
The din of the world disappears in His silence.

During God-remembrance, thou bearest God within thee;
The Most High says: thou wast, thou art, in Me.

LXXV

The heart is made of Truth
In its deepest core.
Within it sings the Sovereign Good
In hours consecrated to God.

Let Truth be the soul's fragrance,
Not worldly din.
Thy heart is the mighty fortress;
Therein dwell Light and Love.

LXXVI

Since thou dost exist, thou must be someone;
Thou canst not be bare existence alone;
Concrete existence is limited "I";
Happy the man who has learnt about the Spirit's Self.

The Spirit can know the illusion of thine egoity,
When it sees that all human beings call themselves "I";
It knows thine I-phenomenon: this is not
The Selfhood that Eternity promises.

The "I" and the Self can meet each other;
The Most High will bless the inner man.
But do not think that the "I" is an empty ruse —
The cosmos mirrors itself just as it is.

God knows thou art in the garment of time —
Whatever thou may'st be, thou art in His hands.

LXXVII

Melancholy, despair, hatred and bitterness,
Nourished by pride and blind self-love —
These are the worst of all the soul's tendencies;
No better is bitter piety

Nourished by pride: hence also by evil;
Whoever opens himself to it, cannot be saved.

LXXVIII

God grant that I may speak of Heaven —
I have often done it and wish to do so endlessly.
I wish to console, yet one cannot always
Rest in the little paradise of gentleness.

Truth is watching. The world is ever the same —
Patience. We are very far from the Kingdom of God.

LXXIX

The Kingdom of God is distant, but only when seen from the outside,
Not within the soul that is open to it.
The eternal is here, it is thy kernel —
Blessèd is he who walks the inward path.

LXXX

A prejudice is idle self-deceit —
One should always strive after the essence of things.
Rigorous thinking has in it something of death:
Desires must die and truth must live.

LXXXI

Him whom thou reverest, fear; him whom thou lovest,
Esteem highly. The one requires the other;
Thou dost accomplish both before thy Lord
In quintessential prayer, when thou givest Him thy heart.

The Lord is disposed to save
What He loves and respects — what He created
As a likeness for immortality.

LXXXII

Haphazardness amongst haphazard things —
This is the human being; necessary he is not.
Necessity belongs to the Lord alone;
He is the rock on which appearances break.

Yet necessity dwells in thy core:
Thou art not empty night; thou art a star —
In thy heart is a greeting from the light of the Sun.

LXXXIII

We live in time; who can rest?
Time is long, we must do something;
For time pursues us. We pursue it,
In the eternal Now — thus time becomes the Never.

LXXXIV

The soul that has become wise
And is no longer attached to things, could be unhappy —
Yet it is happy, since, light and free,
It soars above the heaviness of earthly things.

Between the two states, there may lie something dark —
No bird can fly on the first day.

LXXXV

Happy — but not at every moment:
The world must be experienced, bit by bit.
It is existence, it is not our fault —
The path is truth, humility and patience.

Beatitude: it lies at the bottom of our soul;
And then: it radiates in thee, hour after hour;
In God's Name resounds the benevolence of the Most High.

LXXXVI

We came to sing about God.
From the beginning, the earthly demon
Wanted to destroy us. He was not allowed to succeed —
He had to be content with his ugly snares.

Vexation and to-and-fro belong to life —
Where light is, there has always been shadow.
Many a person has something good to bring to the world —
If it is from God, nothing can defeat him.

LXXXVII

Man's knowledge — it must have limits;
The question is what sets these limits;
For it must lie in the nature of things
And not in the preferences of the human mind.

The principle is that knowledge pertain
To that which leads us to the point rather than to space.
The question as to where lies the balance of the two
Can only be decided by our intellect, with God as its point of departure.

LXXXVIII

Somewhere I read that only he has faith
Who in misfortune, not in happiness, rejoices —
A pious delusion. For everything comes from God;
Not only the injustice that cries to Heaven.

God's Word in the good is direct;
It is indirect in the wrath of His rod.
For in His Essence, God is Love;
Let not Truth's measure be displaced.

LXXXIX

The soul is woven of a thousand questions;
Yet the answer — it is always there;
It dwells within thy breast; be not far from it —
The Most High is ever near.

Say "yes" to God, He will say "yes" to thy heart;
What thou knowest not, He knows; thou hast a share
In this through thy faith. Pronounce it —

In the "yes" from God to God salvation blooms.

XC

What I give to God — it is prefigured
In God's Essence. My poor gift
Is rich through Him. For what God has given me
In His Benevolence is all that I have.

XCI

The spirit, the soul — quite often a to-and-fro,
Because of the world which invades the inward.
Sometimes the co-existence is difficult —

One has lost much strength, much time —
But when God's nearness resounds in the heart,
The soul is born anew through grace.

XCII

Sacred languages: Sanskrit, Hebrew, and
Arabic; languages which have served worship
For more than a thousand years; which to their peoples
Appeared as the expression of the highest heavenly power.

Sacred speech, not only the meaning, but the sound —
The Word, borne by heavenly music.
A magic that penetrates the soul — awakening
Truths that were hidden in the heart.

What the Lord saith to man
Cannot be said in just any way —
Not every manner of speaking reaches God.

XCIII

In Hindu terms, Christ is an example
Of the great *Avatāra* who appears
When men are steeped in sin,
And over every one of whom an angel weeps.

The *Avatāra* — like the great Rama —
Comes to bring anew the *Krita-Yuga*,
And to liberate men. God grant
That over every one of them an angel will once again sing.

XCIV

As is the language, so is the religious form:
The essential content is in each form the same.
What counts is not what the symbols may be —
What counts is that the Message should reach men's hearts.

Because God, the One, sends us the peace of Salvation.
In essence, there is only one Message —
But the Spirit wills to vary the emphasis.

XCV

In the early morning sunshine, thou art who thou art.
Patience — be resigned to the fate
Of always being the same person;

For the world too is always the same world.
Only in the Infinite are there no limitations;
Here below, accept whatever pleases God —

For He stands above all earthly thought.

XCVI

I heard a lute deep in the night —
O sweet sound of a song without words.
Who thought so lovingly of me —
Who, in my dream, stood at my heart's door?

The soul is a veil of dreams, woven
Of longing that yearns for love;
Beauty and love are the melody
My own heart gave me in the night.

The primordial nature of the Good is to overflow —
But its wave, which chose the distant,
Longs to return from the shadows of foreign lands;

And thus was born the secret song
That vibrates through the chords of my soul

And ultimately sprang forth from God's Love.

XCVII

Man is nostalgia for Paradise
       And its light.
Most men are not true to themselves —
       They destroy it.

Matter and selfishness have misled you
       And separated you from the essence
Of primordial Nature; therefore become
       What ye were in God.

If — God willing — we choose the True
       With a sincere disposition
There is a ray of blessing in it
       For all souls.

XCVIII

Time of youth — already past and gone —
Like a picture book that is closed.
All joys, all sorrows have melted away
Into yesterdays.

Time of old age — thou callest it time,
It is rather a quiet garden,
Perfumed by eternity —
A looking back, an awaiting,

And a standing still in That which was,
Is, and shall be — evermore.

XCIX

What is the difference between earth and Heaven —
Between the here-below and the hereafter? Whoever fosters hope
Knows that in this world it is we who bear the work —
Whereas in the next world it is grace that bears us.

The man who sows carries the weight of the seed —
But he need not ask about the harvest.

C

Ye ask for proof of the Highest Being,
And also of Heaven; I have often said
That the criterion lies in consciousness —
For the proof is precisely that ye ask.

CI

In the West I saw Indians riding,
One behind the other: feathered crowns
Blowing in the wind, lances richly adorned —
An image of the path where the spirits dwell.

I was deeply moved by this unusual sight —
I felt that its greatness was outside time,
As if the path were without beginning or end —
The direction that leads to the Great Spirit.

CII

What is greatness in men? When genius
From a divine fountain,
Resounds in any realm of this world,
In any human collectivity.

Not only as a support for what is called "culture";
But also amongst tribes and groups
That remain close to Virgin Nature.

It is as if the essence of things were calling:
Where there is greatness, there is also depth.

CIII

Gypsy, thy violin wept a long time —
It was a love-song without name
That faded away unheard, at the brink of night.

Because thy soul avoided thine own heart,
Thou knewst not whither thou wouldst wander,
And stoodst lonesome as the day took leave.

Until the singing of thy violin told thee
That thou shouldst turn towards thine own depth,
Where all is made complete in the love of God.

CIV

God is the center that reconciles the world
With its meaning, the meaning out of which it arose —
He was a hidden treasure that had to be known;
He transformed Himself into a symbol.

Where is the path to the ultimate center?
May the Lord build for us the golden bridge.
What is the deep meaning for our soul?
Resignation to God — trust in God.

CV

Mount Meru, it is said, is the center
That links our world with Brahma's realm;
But the wise *jivan-mukta* knows
That the Mount is to be found in his heart.

CVI

God gave the earthly pilgrim a bowl
In which He placed many keys;
Let the pilgrim take what his condition likes —
Knowing that there is only One Key.

CVII

The essential nature of the Good wishes to overflow —
But its wave, which chose the distant,
Cannot accustom itself to the foreign world;

And so came into being the nostalgic song
That resounds in the depth of our soul,
And ultimately arose from God's Love.

CVIII

The world exists — but as a changing play;
God-consciousness is absolute.
It bespeaks the One, Sublime Goal —
Salvation, which ever beckoned in thy heart.

So stand before God, and let things come
To thee; think not thou art alone.
Faith and resignation shall avail thee
On thy path —
                    God shall be thy Shepherd.

CIX

Delight in the many, longing for the One:
Mysteries that are emphasized in music and dance —
Amongst Spaniards, Russians and Hungarians —
And combine in an enchanting rapture.

Delight in the many: strength and cheerfulness
Close to nature — far from hollow artificiality.
Then longing for the One: and, from this, the greatness
And depth that liberate us from the petty.

CX

The object of worship is one thing;
The manner and quality of faith is another.
Perhaps someone was only taught a little,
But his faith has the ardor of wine.

Or again, one may be conscious of the Truth
Without drawing the consequences therefrom,
And with a lifeless faith in one's breast;
God grant that His Word may burn our illusion.

Happy the man who deemed a stone to be divine
And whose prayer was performed with humility;
God willed to be present in that stone,
And accepted the faith and the believer.

CXI

The Christmas tree that stood in the center —
A childlike foolishness I would like to forget,
If its deep meaning were not so evident.

I dreamt that I was sitting under its shelter,
In its warmth that evoked Heaven —
Protected as in a golden vessel

With a sweet scent. Meanwhile an angel played the violin
Above the silver star on that tree of wonders,
Which gently bowed before God's nearness.

CXII

The same thing can never repeat itself:
All-Possibility excludes repetition,
Because the latter would limit the former;
The nature of things ordained it thus.

This is certainly true, yet each of us sees
That similar things are forever piercing through time anew;
It is how a thing happens that is not repeatable,
The mode of the event — but not the event itself.

Otherwise time would be a constant changing —
Whereas things are what they are on earth.

CXIII

Space must repeat forms endlessly,
Otherwise there would be only one single form —
But no form is exactly like another,
For only the Essential is the norm.

Thou thinkest one grain of sand is like another —
It only appears so to our sight!
Thou canst not find on earth two identical things,
Otherwise all things would become one.

Two things that were in no wise different
Would be the same in space and time.
And what finally could be unique
Would be one with Infinity.

CXIV

India is Shankara together with Vedanta —
Also Ramanuja, Abhinavagupta,
And Lallā Yōgishvarī; and finally
Tiruválluvar, the holy *pariah*.

Thus India is an entire world;
Characteristic of this world is the Veda's light —
And also the fact that it contains every spiritual perspective.

CXV

"The Opening" — Islam's main prayer —
Asks for devotion and faith in the One;
Then follows refuge — for the believer
Should combine fear of God with love of God.

Worship: that he should bow toward Mecca;
And refuge: that he should turn inward.
Here dwells what is called *As-Sirr*—"the secret,"
Whereof the Sufi is the best witness.

CXVI

Dreaming from my father, energy from my mother —
It was not always easy to combine the two:
To have, in the midst of action, a heavy soul —
To conquer and to weep at the same time.

Then came something from Above, renewing
The soul, overpowering the nightmare;
The two poles became harmony —
A heavenly song penetrated the heart.

CXVII

Think of God as the In-Itself. And then:
Think of God as the Self in our innermost depth.
God as the One, the Unique; and then
God as Union, Self-Remembrance.

Both are One. In God, nothing can be divided;
Divinity within ourselves is knowledge of God.
Whether all-transcending or in-dwelling —
The mind can stress whichever is useful.

Through discernment the mind can grasp many things;
But in the One as such lies Peace —
The one and indivisible Reality.
Primordial Being — deep Self: Beatitude.

CXVIII

Krishna and Christ are two poles of the Spirit:
Both embody Love, but one does so
In beauty and the other in sacrifice.

In heavenly music; and in the wine of grace.

CXIX

Krishna saw his own self — as the Infinite —
In the throng of lovely *gopis*.
They experienced in Krishna, O wonder,
Their own self — but as the Absolute.
And when, in play, he stole their veils,
He wished to see himself in Truth's naked ray.

Ātmā and *Māyā*: light and mirror.
God is Love and He loves His image.

CXX

There were some priests who scolded a yogi:
Canst thou not keep the rules of the *dharma*?
He replied: the *dharma* is in the word Om;
Why should I unfold the Infinite?

CXXI

Just as the Lord radiated the world
Without departing from His Essence —
So may man look upon the outward,
But he must strive toward the inward;

Then may thy spirit gaze into thy soul,
And, true to itself, bridge the distance —
It confers on thy soul the meaning of existence.

Certainly the Lord can live without creation —
But without God, thou canst not lift a finger.

CXXII

It is said: wisdom is to know
That the Lord is the Doer. But my doing
Was allotted to me by God, and indeed often commanded —
Otherwise I might remain dreaming and doing nothing.

God willed that there be a creature who acts;
Otherwise He would not have made us men.
Certainly, without Him, no action would be possible —
Nevertheless He ordained freedom for us.

CXXIII

How is it that God acts in human beings?
It is through the God-created faculties,
And also in the play of the soul's possibilities.
It is not God who acts in sin,
Nor in the good that we prepare for ourselves.
It is not for nothing that we pray that God forgive.

Man's actions are not blind like lead;
I act, because it is God's wish that I do so.

CXXIV

What matters is not — some have said —
That thou lovest God, but rather that God loves thee.
Why so? What God feels is not my concern;
What is needful is that I dominate my inclinations.

Who is it that God loves? I do what I can
And wish to do, for the good. That is what matters.

CXXV

God is the One, He alone is; thus proclaims Islam.
From this came the tendency
To attribute absolutely everything to the Most High —
What is lacking here is wisdom's sieve;
This comes from God. One should not exaggerate.

There is the freedom of outward actions;
There is the freedom that teaches us how to think —
This is the nature of the Intellect, it is not merit.
Knowledge is free, because it belongs to God.

CXXVI

In Islam, music was at first proscribed;
To the Koran alone might one turn one's ear.
But Rūmī brought music into the house of Islam,
With the ecstatic circle of dance.

In primitive Islam, sobriety was the bearer of grace;
But the power of grace pierced the silence,
And became music, in order to move hearts.

Chivalrous poetry too was put to silence;
Jalāl ad-Dīn sang only of God.

CXXVII

Man is the image of God, but the Lord
Should not appear to you in the image of man.
Furthermore: do not say that only will
And sentiment can unite us with God.
And finally: truth is not fanaticism
That does injustice to every foreign faith.

Do not reject knowledge, the pure intellect,
That shows us the way to God's Nature —
And lies within our own nature.

CXXVIII

The blasphemer thinks: if God exists,
He must let the philosophers doubt;
For what is called God's Revelation,
Cannot be grasped by human reason.

They know not that God dwells in man's heart
And, so to speak, thinks within us —
They know not that He rewards man's openness with light.

CXXIX

It has been said that there is no greater sin
Than that of our existence. A saying of the Prophet —
What does it mean? Did not God
Place us in this life?

Existence as such is remote from God,
But not as the meaning of our earthly life:
The Path to the Most High through prayer —

Only One Power raises us up to the One.

CXXX

Excess lies in human nature;
Hence the to-and-fro of history.
God grant that men do not ruin too much —
May God's Wrath not destroy the world.

The Pope was the overlord of religion;
The emperors' attitude was in defiance of this;
Yet — according to Dante — they were right;
The Guelph-pope was a slave of vile avidity.

It is possible that even the enemy of the good
Can be right in certain circumstances,
Because hypocritical habit ruins many things —
The path to perfection is steep.

CXXXI

Thou shouldst not cling obstinately, without measure,
To shifting thoughts — be still
Before God. The past is gone; and what
Lies before thee, is what the Most High wills.

CXXXII

Dialectic and music — since my earliest days
I have carried both faithfully within me.
The first as a starting-point for the True,
The other as a path to the Miraculous.

CXXXIII

The river: a path from non-existence to the All;
From the source to the ocean — there is nothing more.

After the roar of a waterfall
It flows, renewed, into the sea.

And likewise man: after the crisis of a trial,
He awakens blissfully on Heaven's meadow.

CXXXIV

The Virgin said: they have no wine.
This means: one would be right to take joy in the wedding.
The soul's happiness may also be of this earth.
As long as one understands: the Kingdom is within.

May earthly happiness also be heavenly.

CXXXV

"There is no victor except God":
This is written on the Alhambra's walls.
Defeats betoken the world;
The final victory is in the Hands of the Most High.

If, amidst thy cares, thou thinkest of God,
Then God's victory is hidden in thy Word,
In the Supreme Name, which forgives thy being —
A draught of approaching Infinity.

CXXXVI

Several lives, but within one life —
This was my path; and within it, several deaths;
And may God grant — since I have seen so much —
That others may inherit my message.

And ask not who I am. For every striving
On High is given by the Holy Spirit.

CXXXVII

Peace and joy are the two poles
Of happiness conferred by God's Truth;
They are the two paradisal gardens
Of the human soul that loves the True.

Peace comes when the afflicted soul
Serenely soars above its cares;
And joy: when, full of divine solace,
It strives inward, away from the world.

Certitude of God and serenity
Above the din of the world, this is bliss.

CXXXVIII

God's Truth radiates beauty —
Thou livest from beauty just as thou livest from the word
Of Truth that ordained the whole universe
And willed each symbol in its proper place.

There is no wisdom without noble meaning;
There is no beauty that bespeaks not God;
The essence of nobility strives towards the Truth.

The true will awaken love of God —
Depth of beauty will unite with God.

In thy depth thou wilt find the Most High.

Songs without Names

Third Collection

The stream of songs already wished to stop;
And I too wished to end the stream.
But the Spirit willed to continue turning the pages.
And I could not keep to my intention.
What the Spirit willed, I was obliged to write.

Songs without Names

Third Collection

I

Motionless center, outside time,
In God's presence. The world-wheel
Knows no halt, but thou see'st it not,
For the Spirit put thee in the center,

Yet thou art in existence, and must live with other men,
Thou must enter into the play of the world-wheel,
And from thence must strive toward the center.

This is thy fate; the space of existence is vast —
Within thy heart Eternity keeps watch.

II

In the beginning God said: "Let there be light!"
Let these words be thine answer.
Thou art in the darkness of this earthly world —
Be thou, in it, Divinity's reflection.

The *Fiat Lux* means: "I am That I am."
Thou repeatest it, and at the same time
It is an answer: I am not — only Thou, Lord, art.
And this, O man, is the meaning of thine existence.

III

Space is infinite, and so is time —
Infinity cannot be grasped by reason.
We must let ourselves be borne
By All-possibility through our earthly existence.

We do not know what space and time are —
We only know that they prove Being.
For, since they are — one thing is certain:
In bowing down, they circle around God.

IV

To be "I" is to relate all things
To one viewpoint. Quite other is Knowledge:
For it relates the "I" to pure Being,
And ultimately cannot separate it from God.

Pure Knowledge mirrors Ipseity,
And is its Selfhood, immutable.

V

The Creator clothed the wide world
In a garment of enigmas;
Beauty seeks to pierce the illusion of existence,
Just as a meteor cuts through the night.

Truth, a ray of the Godhead,
Has rent the darkness of our soul;
Happy the one in whose heart the light of the Most-High
Reigns like a ray of the morning sun.

VI

Being has power, it can negate Itself —
Non-being cannot stand on its own feet.
Paradox: nothingness as such is nothing —
But mixed with existence, it is the shadow of a light.

VII

When God's Name resounds in thy consciousness
Together with God's Presence — then be ready:
Then thou standest on the ground of Eternity,
And askest not what the morrow brings.

VIII

Whether I be here below, or above
In the better hereafter, is the same for God;
At one moment on earth, and then in Paradise —
Whoever prays sincerely, is in God's kingdom.

The turmoil of the world has no power —
Man is made as the mirror of God.

IX

One kind of God-remembrance is solemn and grave;
Another is light like the song of a lark.
Be like a rock, be like a spring breeze —
Both belong to the music of thy soul.

There is the man who saves his soul
Because, with effort, he vanquishes its illusions.
A people will come, said the Prophet,
Who, like a lark, will ascend to Heaven.

X

The archetype, breaking through the naught,
Gives rise to Beauty, lent to us by God;
See how the wonders contained within Divinity,
Pass before our sight in this world

To remind us of a mystery:
The meaning of Beauty is the way to the Inward.

XI

Is it not strange that to beauty
There also belongs a gentle grief? The summer night
Brought the love song of the nightingales,
A song of longing, into my heart.

Tell me, O sweet night — tell me
Why longing must burn in our soul.
Because, banished to this earthly vale,
We cannot forget a distant glowing —

The bliss that we have known in God.

XII

The truth, the whole truth, and nothing but the truth —
Thus one has to swear in court.
God-remembrance
Is the same: if thou standest before God's Face,
Thou must give Him thy whole soul.

XIII

What is evil? Not a second being,
But impossibility becoming possible.
All-possibility comprises this enigma —
Being was ready for its own negation.

Evil lies in the way one sees things, someone said,
And not in the thing itself — thus truth becomes smaller.
Certainly, evil can lie in the way one sees things —
But this is no reason to lie about the being of things.

It also has been said, good is what God wills;
Not so. Good is God's Nature — and our goal.

XIV

I cannot stand within existence
Otherwise than how God has willed me: this ego,
And no other. But in the Self
I am pure Being, where all the earthly world has vanished.

XV

Reality: God is first, and alone.
In thine everyday life, let Him be first in thy consciousness.
God was always there; be not far from Him —
He is always near thee.

XVI

There are different degrees of union
With God in the hereafter; but man retains
The possibility of his I-consciousness,
Both in Paradise with God and in the earthly world.

Already here on earth, the human soul
Has two dimensions. In the Divinity thou see'st
The Essence and the Names.
Eternity: in the Divinity too, thou art what thou art.

XVII

"State" and "station" — *hāl, maqām* —
Mysteries named by the Sufi Masters:
The first is what may come by chance;
The second is the deep knowledge of the heart.

Do not confuse them: for the emotion
Caused by an experience is not
An intrusion of Eternity into the soul —
It is not a lasting, bestowed light.

XVIII

On the one hand, meditation:
This is contemplation of what you know;
On the other hand, concentration:
This is absorption in the Spirit which is.

On these two God-given paths,
The soul should move toward the Most High.

XIX

Do not do several things at once;
Do one thing after the other, as the dignity
Of things, and of thyself, demands —
Therefore be orderly, and make thy choice.
Even God allotted to each day its burden,
When He created things without number.

Thou canst not sow different things at the same time;
For every seed wills to be wholly itself.

XX

Promise not more than thou canst keep;
Nor keep less than thou hast promised —
"A man is as good as his word" is an old saying.
No noble man ever broke his word —
He would thereby have broken with himself.

Promise, and keep, thy faithfulness to the Most High,
So that thou mayst live without blemish or remorse;
Just as He keeps what He has promised:
Through His Name and for thy Path.

XXI

Faithfulness — a quality of gold —
What would God-Remembrance be without faithfulness?
It is the unfettered strength of life,
It leads us from narrowness to luminous space.
Whatever be the play of our earthly existence —
Live thou in God, and thus be true to thyself.

Faithfulness in God's Will never wavers —
With the Most High, the Now is the Ever.

XXII

One would gladly live without the evil one
But God has given him the right to exist,
If it were not so, the earthly world would be Heaven;
Honor is due to pure Being alone.

The serpent was already in Paradise —
We fell, but God never abandoned us.

XXIII

Every happiness is a distant ray
Of the one, indivisible Bliss;
But let not thy happiness be mere symbol.

The path to the Highest Good is far —
Participation in this happiness on earth
Belongs only to the heart that has experienced God.

But also in pure, noble, small things,
Thou hearest from afar the angel of the Most High sing,
And thou hearest thine own heart in its song.

The song of bliss is Peace, Peace.

XXIV

Within my heart the weary day is singing —
With the last rays of the sun, its drink is bowing down.
The cool, nostalgic night draws nigh —
An angel plays on a golden violin.

What does the sun's last ray wish to tell us?
That on earth we carry, in the depth of our soul,
A nostalgia for Paradise —

And God grant that it may show us the way.

XXV

Paradise is the highest value for the soul,
For it contains everything the heart desires.
You may ask me: what is Paradise?
A place of joy? It is infinitely more.

XXVI

"Praise the Lord" — what does this mean?
It is for us, God does not need it for Himself.
It means: we should know what God is eternally,
In Heaven and on earth.

To know is to become — to become what God intended
When He put spirit and soul into clay —
The Lord, who needs nothing outside Himself,
Breathed Himself into the nothingness of heavy earth.

XXVII

Life, it is said, is a movement towards death;
Not so — life flows towards God alone.
One hardly says that one goes only to the door,
When one could be a guest of the King.

What comes before death, is God's Will;
What comes after, is the fullness of His Grace.

XXVIII

Death: no one can reach pure Being
If he has not gone through the door of nothingness.
Life and death: neither of them counts
Before our goal — or before God's Countenance.

XXIX

Non-Being: this is synonymous with nothingness.
But for some "Non-Being" is Beyond-Being,
Primordial Being, All-possibility — the Principle of Being;
The quintessence of the Highest Light.

What is a word? How should things be named?
One has to know different ways of expression.

XXX

All the images of the world rush into thee
Through the five doors of thy senses —
But if thou closest thine eyes, and also those of thy soul,
Thou art in the quiet tent of the Spirit.

So let not thyself be seduced by any dream
That earthly *Māyā* wants to offer —
Either from outside or from within thine own soul.

Life's din is loud — the Spirit is silence.

XXXI

If thou protect the Lord in thy heart,
He will protect thee here on earth.
And likewise: thou shouldst meet thy Lord
Already here-below; He will bless thee in the Hereafter —

So that the meaning of existence be fulfilled.
Manifestation of God, for the Good wishes to give;
Return to God — there is no other life.

XXXII

Birth and death — two shores, and a sea
Between them we must cross;
Whence comest thou, O man, and whither dost thou go?
Who will greet thee at thy long journey's end?

Birth and God — the path from nothingness to Being;
Nothingness, Existence, Being — thou art tossed upon
The waves of existence, everything seems to sway.
But the boat is drawn towards God by the hand of Grace.

XXXIII

In reality, the path to God is not a movement —
It is a timeless abiding in the center.
Thou standest there and askest: Who am I?
Be not concerned. An angel moves for thee.

XXXIV

When thou directest thy steps, O man,
Forget not that thou becomest what thou thinkest.
Think of what shines down on thee from Above —
And then of what the Most High has written in thy heart.

XXXV

God is Love — and therefore God is Life.
Being's radiation gives life; life testifies to Being.
Nothingness is but a symbol, it has no value in itself;
The appearance of illusion pertains to possibility.

That which is not can add nothing to that which is;
In the play of existence the honor is to the Lord.

Nothingness cannot falsify God's Wine.

XXXVI

An angel spoke: thou shouldst not be sad;
God is the Absolute and the Sovereign Good.
And then: because everything that troubles thee
In this world, rests in His Hands.

XXXVII

In God's Essence shines a silent Light
Within a circle of unfathomed marvels.
This shining — but thy soul knows it not —
Art thou, before and after all earthly times.

XXXVIII

Vishnu and Lakshmi — lofty powers
That conceive and weave and penetrate the world;
Here is Light, and with it Love —
See how messengers from Heaven bring us radiance and warmth.

Wisdom and Beauty — Plato's words.
May the Lord guide thee on both paths.
They resound together deeply in world and heart.

XXXIX

The naïvety of former times is quite astounding —
How easily one thundered at one's interlocutor.
One made no effort to understand
What, fundamentally, the other sought to say —
One could not see one's own self in the other.

Certainly, mankind cannot become more intelligent —
Nevertheless experience does exist on earth.

XL

In the church there is holy water,
And incense is also used;
See how water can be blessed,
And how fragrance rises to Heaven.

Ganges water purifies
From sin, and so does the water of baptism;
To the Great Spirit rises the smoke
Of the Pipe, and breathes life into the wind.

Water purifies the soul,
Wine transmutes thee into spirit.
Water is for everyone —
He who can comprehend it, drinks the Wine.

XLI

Consecrated water and consecrated wine —
Signs of the sacraments; bread, oil,
And other vehicles of grace — nourishment
For the soul imprisoned in earthly illusion.

But it is true — thou mayest ask thy heart —
That we carry the source of grace within us.
No holy water on earth can purify more
Than the deeply inward water of Knowledge.

XLII

With sacred formulas — mantras — one can depict
God's image — an edifice of numbers;
This is a pious illusion, for the mantra itself is an image;
In it, the Divinity's wish has been fulfilled.

XLIII

Dante's language makes Latin milder;
Alongside Shankara, there must be Ramanuja.
Analogously: after the Highest Reality,
The personal God is ready to help man.

Truth, Serenity, way of Knowledge;
And then God's goodness, and the ardor
Of the human soul in response to grace —
Sacrificial love for the Highest Good.

Shankara could also sing of beauty —
Thomas could bring wisdom into love;
See how the wheel of the Spirit turns.

XLIV

The sexual parts — in the West they are an image of sin,
They are veiled, because they show Adam's shame;
In India they are often uncovered and revered —
Gods, before whom the faithful bow:
Purusha and *Prakriti* — male and female;
Thus is polarized the creative ray of Brahma.

Earthly ambiguity and misery — but at the same time:
Heavenly archetype in the realm of the Spirit.

XLV

There is a mysticism of love, which lives from sacrifice;
So the Apostle Paul. And there is a mysticism of knowledge,
As Plato taught, which tends toward beauty.

Forget not the breadth of Divine Truth:
Each spiritual way partakes of the other —
On every side thou findest the Good.

XLVI

A prince gives a castle to a saint;
The saint gives this gift to a poor man —
"I have nothing else," he tells him, and he thinks:
This is how one shows pity for one's neighbor.

Does this tale bear witness to the highest virtue?
Exaggeration destroys the value.
In fact, the pious fool deceived
Two other people besides himself.

Senseless was the prince's giving,
Senseless was the other's receiving.
One has to say it, but one hardly dares:
The dreams of blind faith make one stupid.

XLVII

The Sufis, even more than the Christians,
Lived in a dream-world of symbols —
They thought that, in the dry reality
Of the everyday world, there was nothing spiritual to be found.

The holy fool shrinks from nothing, as long as,
In his actions, the spirits of mystical teaching shine forth.

XLVIII

A book about the Sufis of Andalusia:
Miracles come as profusely as rain —
When a pious man wishes for anything,
He only has to move his finger.

Religion is an entire world.
Be not astonished that much falls from Heaven —
At its blossom time, but not in our time
Of decline, which cries to Heaven.

XLIX

A saint weeps over his sins —
His tears flow over the threshold
In a stream. It would have been better, it seems to me,
If he had shed tears for something else.

Ye pious writers, do not exaggerate —
Make not the weight too heavy on the scales.
Thus it is with men — both Moslems and Christians —
For whom the will is more than wisdom.

L

Exegesis of the Holy Scriptures: take care
That thine efforts do not disrespect the literal meaning;
Certainly thy mind may plumb the depths —
But it must not go beyond God's intention.

Exegesis, when dragged by the forelock,
Somehow contorts Wisdom's meaning.

LI

Religion — on the one hand it is God,
One wants to garland it with love and awe.
But on the other hand, religion is man —
With his egoity and limitations.

The naked Truth is infinitely precious;
It is hidden behind *Māyā's* veil —
If God wills, it will shine unveiled.

LII

Why should I not revere the sun?
St. Francis also sang its praises.
In the moon's gentle light, when the day has ended,
The sun smiles through a veil.

Sunrise, which gilds the earth,
Reminds us of the light and victory of Truth;
The rising and setting of the sun tells us that the light
Is not its own, but originates in Divinity.

A symbol is everything that shows us greatness —
But only before God does the spirit bow.

LIII

On this poor earth, greatness demands
Cruel reality — but fortunately
Art, which reproduces greatness and transposes it,
Leads us back to the archetype —

To the deep purpose of all earthly things.
May their timeless song resound for our heart
In the arts — in poetry, dance and music.

LIV

Poetry, music, and dance — these arts
Can be either spiritual or worldly:
The worldly man they pull towards worldly enjoyments,
In the spiritual man, they enter into his heart.

Poetry is like music, but it includes thought;
Music inebriates the soul's substance;
In dance, music, transmuted into form,
Becomes the life of the body — it is wine made visible.

LVI

Some say that, with God, knowledge
Derives from the will; they understand badly.
For others, the will is seen to derive from knowledge,
For God is wisdom; they understand rightly.

God is consciousness, therefore He can will;
Selfhood is not the fruit of willing.
Theologians who call God "will,"
Fail to grant precedence to the Divine Intellect alone.

This is because, for them, morality is foremost —
Be careful how ye judge the Highest Wisdom!

LVII

Ye may be astonished that in the mysticism
Of love there is a spark of pride —
The overestimation of one's own experience,
For which, however, God forgives the lover.

LVIII

The *Avatāra* must have two souls:
One for everybody, and one for the intellect
Of the wise. One that converts the world,
And one that shows the way within —

And so teaches us about the limitless One.

LIX

Position in society is one thing,
And deepest inward nature is another.
Everywhere man can be noble —
Birth is often merely name and color.

Thus Tiruválluvar, who is honored;
And so too the *shudra* before whom Shankara bowed.

LX

In Islam it is said that hell does not last forever,
That a cool wind will one day blow through the fire —
And that the damned will finally no longer burn.

They will know the grace of forgiveness —
Mercy is like an immense ring;
The Koran says: "It encompasseth everything."

LXI

In the guilds of earlier times
There was a general and strict custom:
Not only should the work be perfect,
Nobility of soul was also required.

Virtue added value to the work;
Craftsmanship favored inward perfection.

LXII

What in Sanskrit is called *tamas*,
In Arabic is called *waswas*, "whisperer":
The darkness that men carry within themselves —
It cannot be otherwise on this low earth.

The serpent was present in the first Paradise
When our world was in its prime,
And Heaven was still joined to earth —

For to be stained is the price of existence.
But thou art free — may thy heart be the *Pilar*

On which the immaculate Virgin stands.

LXIII

Some take their stand on the ground of faith,
Others on the ground of knowledge;
Some see virtue as obedience,
Others see it as domination of self;
What for believers is theology,
Is for gnostics philosophy —
Not what wrong-thinking names thus,
But what separates error from truth.

LXIV

Imagine that thou hast a pain
In thy heart, and that thou grievest bitterly —
All the things that otherwise would gladden
And console thee are still there, they surround thee,
And wait till thou art grateful.

LXV

Thou hesitatest before the sword of the Highest Truth —
Thou fearest that wisdom may rob thee of thy being,
Thou, who art not. What must come, will come —
And it is God. In Him thou shalt not want.

LXVI

Kaleidoscope — a children's toy,
But also an image of our soul:
A fleeing-from and a chasing-after
That forget the meaning of existence.

The soul builds itself a world from fragments,
And divides into pieces what it has experienced.
See thou, O heart, things as they are —
Eternity within a single instant.

LXVII

There are three kinds of giving: the first
Is sacrifice, expiation, purification and equilibrium;
The second is enrichment —
A radiation that breaks the ice of hearts.

The third giving is squandering —
It comes from the evil one, it is fundamentally a stealing,
A way from nothingness to nothingness. Blessèd are those
Who wisely choose the way from good to good.

The good gives itself back. Whoever gives good
To the thirsty, has given drink to himself.

LXVIII

A woman gives birth to a child: if it is a son —
The father rejoices beyond measure;
But if the little child is a daughter
He often walks through the streets with somber looks,
And is not, for all that, a villain.
Such is man — comprehensible he is not.

People complain about destiny's blows —
Happiness requires gratitude and love.

LXIX

It is often said that even in evil there is some good.
This is more false than true. The end of the story
Is that the substance of a thing drowns out the accident —
The bad annihilates the speck of good.

Nevertheless: when the substance is good,
Then the good — which loves the Most High — will triumph;
For this lies in its very nature. And this
Is proven by the miracle that God forgives us.

LXX

Let the dead bury their dead,
Thus spake Jesus. This means: when thou standest
Before God in prayer, do not think of the messengers
Of the world — otherwise thou wilt not know whither thou goest.

Do not say: before following God's call,
I will turn in another direction.
Certainly, thou must do what reason commands;
But never close the eye of thy heart.

LXXI

It is a pity that one persists in
Worldly thinking — gladly and not so gladly.
Before the door of thy thinking, place a light,
High and serene like the morning star.

Thou shouldst see God before thou losest thyself
In the meander of thy psychic world;
He is the rock, before which the play of the waves
Surges up, then falls away into naught.

LXXII

Formerly it was believed that the sun and
The stars circled round the earth,
And one understood the deep meaning of this appearance.
Today one knows better, but one is no longer wise.

One no longer knows that, in the framework of the universe,
The spirit of man is the true center;
The world, in its way, was a reflected image.

LXXIII

Science: what counts is not what
Man knows about the many things
Contained in the universe; what counts is
What man makes of his detailed knowledge.

For science does not build the house of wisdom —
It is assimilation by the spirit that constitutes wisdom.

LXXIV

It is said of a pseudo-philosopher —
I would rather say of a "misosopher" —
That his rhetoric is so sharp
That no other thinker can surpass him.

A nonsense. For though the speech of madness
Can be powerful, what counts is what one says.
The sage who brings the highest wisdom
Cannot be outdone by even the most cunning speaker.

And this sage will never be alone —
There cannot be only one messenger of Truth.

LXXV

"A universal demolisher": people called the pedant
Who subjected reason to a "critique."
If man's mental faculties have such fissures,
Then so does the phantom that flew through his brain.

It has also been said, there is no truth —
Whereby these words themselves turn to dust.

LXXVI

Relativity as a theory
Sounds important — but it can prove nothing.
One cannot upturn the whole universe
On the pretext that bodies move
Without a unifying relationship to a center.

Motion faster than the speed of light
Is no longer measurable, it amounts to nothing —
God grant that no one quarrel over this.

LXXVII

Birds that cry out the Supreme Name,
May well be happy after death;
Not so men who recite the Name
And within their souls have pride and hatred.
The call "Lord, Lord" of vain evil-doers
Destroys all the blessing of this act.

LXXVIII

It is lamentable that so many people
Carry all kinds of opinions in their heads —
Judgments that distort their souls —
And do not think of the rights of truth.

One must learn how to think correctly,
Instead of limiting one's mind to wishful thinking.
An error — even when apparently insignificant —
Can be harmful for oneself and others.

According to San Juan: from the devil come those thoughts
That are like rocks, yet suffer from falseness —
Aping what the pure Intellect
Awakens in our soul as certitude.

LXXIX

The unnatural is also natural,
There is no difference between them.
In saying this, the culprit seeks to wash his hands
Of his sins — always the same old story.

Certainly what happens must happen;
This has always been the way of things.
But the fact that, in the world, there is such a thing as fate,
Does not annul the difference just referred to.

Being is Being. One cannot say otherwise:
All-Possibility must contain contradictions;
Because it gives, even to nothingness,
Something of its abundance, which loves to give.

LXXX

An over-clever man once wrote:
We do not love that which manifests beauty,
But we consider beautiful that which we love.

If what men love capriciously is beautiful,
This would mean that beauty does not exist.

LXXXI

We do not believe what is true, a creature wrote,
But, on the contrary, truth is what we believe.
In other words: truth does not exist —
The fox disdains the grapes that are beyond his reach.

LXXXII

False science has no limits,
For it will not recognize the Pure Intellect.
If it knew the Intellect, it would also know:
Only God is the ultimate goal of knowledge.

LXXXIII

I must speak of many different things,
Because all too few love what is great —
Because all too many in the world become stupid.
I would prefer to give a deeper teaching:

Concerning the things that awaken in your consciousness
The Truth of the Most High, and the steps of the Path.

LXXXIV

Genius is nothing, if not combined with nobility and piety.
Better to be naïve like children,
Single-minded and in God —
Not mental fireworks and at the same time miserably split.

Do not forget the judgment of God:
Truth is everything — a superman is nothing.

LXXXV

One can be so objective, without prejudice
Or egoism, that one burns oneself up;
But there is the God-given knowledge
That lies in thy heart; it is of the highest worth,
Because it is weightier by far than what thy thinking can do:

The certainty that what reigns over all things
Also dwells within thy heart —
A Spring that belongs to God and never dries up.

LXXXVI

Existence is like walking on a mountain:
First and foremost uphill — this is spiritual effort;
But also downhill — this is the life of the body.

Both together: uphill, and within it, downhill;
An intertwining from birth to death —

And may God raise us to His Heights.

LXXXVII

First the Name of God: presence
Of the Sovereign Good; then the many-sided wisdom
That the Name contains; and then,
Concerning thee: domination of thyself;
And finally the grace-filled world of beauty.

LXXXVIII

There are rare people, who as children
Were like old men, because they had an intuition of Wisdom,
And who in old age become younger

Without the exhortation of others.
Pneumatikós: such a one knows that Eternity
Is hidden in things; and that in the heart

The immutable miracles of God resound.

LXXXIX

The *Virgen del Pilar* possesses a robe
That was designed by the poet of this book —

Heaven wills that from time to time
This grace-filled image shine according to our spirit.

XC

We are in this world to manifest
Words of truth and the circle of our spiritual way.
Say not that we know not this or that —
If we but know that the Lord knows it.

XCI

When did stillness lay itself upon the song?
The circle is without beginning and without end —
A movement that expands and goes forth
Towards the inward — and closes in God's Hands.

XCII

Two values are consoling — I wish to say anew —
Certitude of God and trust in God.
One in the spirit, the other in the soul —
Thou canst, and must, rely on both these values.

XCIII

Man is created to be a god,
And yet he's but a helpless earthly being,
Indeed even an animal. He lives divided within himself
And wishes to be liberated from this contradiction,

And he cannot — except in those hours
When all oppositions are transcended in God.

XCIV

When an experience — be it of beauty or of greatness —
Deeply moves thee, seek not to explain it;
Forget the form in God, in its archetype —
Then thou wilt hear its profound message.

XCV

Leave behind thoughts that plague thee needlessly;
The world should bear its illusion on its own.
Thou shouldst not fight with worldly thoughts —
Let them slip into nothingness before the Lord.

Be ever ready for the Essential —
The word of Truth is outside time.

XCVI

Seeing, a priori, is always "towards the outside":
Our gaze goes forth of itself towards the outward.
The world is what it is; if you wish to see it,
You go out and interact with things —

Unless you know that, in order to see
The deep Essence, you must look within yourself.

Say not that the science of the outward is false,
Because it sees things only from without;
"To see from within" is to ask much —
First explain this, so that you be understood.

XCVII

That our earth goes round the sun,
And at the same time turns on its axis,
Had to be discovered, sooner or later —

But this discovery was the source of error for philosophers.
Previously, the sun's path had been a symbol:
It demonstrated that phenomena are transient —

That only the Most High is everlasting.

XCVIII

One must beware of sensory and mental illusions,
When making an objective investigation;
In such matters, the scientist is entirely right —
But he is not right when he thinks that the Intellect can be dispensed with,
As if the sage were but a dreamer;
Knowledge is deception, when the Intellect is not the center.

The truth is that pure objectivity is necessary —
And with it the whole Self, not merely the half;
The essential Self which sees all that is real —
The Light of Eternity.

XCIX

World-murderers I would call those fools
Who, full of science up to their ears,
Have only one concern in their heads:
That people should not desert their goal of progress.

In the end, their gifts are worthless —
Intelligence without God is suicidal.

C

Why is hell compared with fire?
The soul, suspended between all and nothing,
Despairs, because it has forgotten its meaning —
Because it has overlooked the Sovereign Good.

The human soul is a holy shrine,
Created to be itself only in God.

CI

For Dante, all wise heathens
Were indeed in hell, but in a cool place;
They had not the Christian view of God,
But they rested blissfully before the gate of the Most High.
Here the poet saw Aristotle —
His master — Plato and Socrates;
Saladin, the Moslem, was also in this cool brightness,
And not in the heat of hell.
It was a place, said Dante: *di fresca verdura;*
Genti v'eran con occhi tardi e gravi,
Di grande authorità ne' lor sembianti:
Parlavan rado, e con voci soavi.

CII

Paradise knows no icy cold —
A warm, mild spring breeze blows there;
Nor did the Lord allow a desert heat,
In the land where the saved souls dwell.

God allotted the air of His Goodness to their souls;
In God-remembrance it already blows here below.

CIII

In Hades there is a river called "Lethe";
It makes people forget what they experienced.
At the moment of death, the veil of the images
Woven by destiny will be removed.

But after death, the Lord, in His goodness,
Will give us back the spring songs of the soul.

CIV

Existence: constructed of a thousand things —
Knowledge must bring the world to Unity.
Infallible knowing is the Pure Intellect,
Through which thou, in contemplating, mayst know of the Godhead,
On which the meaning of all things is based —
A Messenger of God said: only God is good.

God intended the universe as manifestation —
As witness to this, man was made.

CV

Men who have no true center
Are but dream-veils; they pass through life
Aimlessly and haphazardly — why, whither?
Then, like autumn leaves, they are gone with the wind.

Forget not, traveler, thou belong'st not to thyself —
Did not the Lord say, when creating thee: thou art Mine!

CVI

One should never believe in what is past —
So said a philosopher from the land of the Ganges.
Truth must be discovered for oneself —
So turn the screws of idle thought.

Truth, says this man, is the creation of one's own mind;
What others say is but an empty seeming;
All this — he says — you have to ponder thoroughly.
That he should tell this to others is incomprehensible.

CVII

In the range of all possible thoughts
One thing alone is absolute: the Most High.
And then the way in which thou understandest this:
The enlightening theme of meditation comes next.

The Supreme Name and the theme of meditation —
These are the golden keys to Eternity.
Truth and then the Path — there is nothing more.
The life of Truth is immortality.

CVIII

Solitude is the lot of the sage, because
He is not as others are. Yet his "I"
Is richer and vaster than so many souls;
The sage carries the whole world within himself.

In a sense he has experienced all things,
Though, in reality, they were not his destiny.
The nature of things lies in his blood —
In the multitude of creatures, he is the archetype.

CIX

What, in my youth, was cruelly real,
Became music in later years —
It became more than the early suffered realities;
An experience from out of eternity.

The fountain of false reality ran dry —
The dream was derided, but the dream was victorious.

CX

Thou hast said God's Name a thousand times,
And so doing, thou hast said it only once.
God-consciousness can only be unique —
The Highest Reality knows not number.
What then is the merit of faithful repetition?
To sow God's blessing in the world.

CXI

Thou canst not fill a cup that is full —
Therefore the soul must be empty during prayer;
When the depth of the heart is the container,
The soul is all the more in need of Lethe.

Vacare Deo is the best drink —
With thy silence, give thanks to the Most High.

CXII

Truths that do not change
Are always there; if I am conscious of this,
I know that I am in God's Hands —
That everything is founded on our sense of the True.

The world has shadows — but be of good cheer
In the face of the Sovereign Good.

CXIII

Hades was the dark unknown —
One did not know exactly what to think of it.
Elysion was certain: the Divinity's wish
Is to bestow eternal peace on noble souls —

For it lies in the nature of the Olympians
That Light finally conquers night.

CXIV

It is important, not only that thou believest in God,
But also that this makes thee happy.
God-consciousness should equally be trust in God —
In melancholy thou art not awakened to God.

Certainly, an earthly thing can sadden thee —
But not for too long; thou must practice meditation.

CXV

Often thou hast fought the past —
Stay where thou art, and see what lies before thee!

Now is future, future is now —
Happy the man who treasures God's last word!

CXVI

It will pass — how often canst thou say this!
It means that thou hast patience and trust in God —
It means that thou standest high on a golden chariot,
And canst look down on earthly life.

How often something has been dark and sad —
Of all of this thou art healed in God.

CXVII

It must be so: there are the different religions —
In which of these houses wilt thou dwell?
Be not confused by the flood of concepts —
Truth is one. And only God is good.

In the beginning, the Word penetrated into us —
The Light is one, but it has many reflections.

CXVIII

Exaggeration, even pious lies —
The end sanctifies the means; nevertheless,
All things have their limits, including pious illusions;
One no longer knows where to turn.

And so truth becomes poetry —
Does this please the Lord? I do not know.
Maybe yes, maybe no; God measures the meaning of the images.

CXIX

After nearly two thousand years
The altars in the churches were turned around,
Thus disfiguring a maternal face;
Mother Church — one can no longer recognize her.

Similar things occurred in other areas —
One no longer knows in which house to dwell
Since the innovators mowed down the sacred customs.

One should pray to God, not to the people.

CXX

We do not criticize the good missionary
Because through his preaching the words of Christ resound;
We criticize him because, at the same stroke,
He brings with him the world of deadly machines,
And diabolical ugliness —
Not the paradisal fragrance of Eternity.

It is painful to mention earthly misery —
For the longing of our soul breathes something different.

CXXI

Miserable are philosophers
When they try to explain to us
What the world is, and why —
And what and how we should think.

For this we have long known,
From the sages of old.
All that is new is that one must
Impart it to new men.

All these little minds are proud
Of their free-thinking comedy;
Each one believes that he alone
Has hit the mark.

But on the Day of Judgment, one will hear:
He know nothing, who knows not God.

CXXII

When people engage in something shameful
Before the whole world, they call it "courage";
The good, they call "prejudice" —
Ripe are the hypocrites for the fire of hell.
It is certain that there must be a hell,
For one can see it in the hellish life of men.

CXXIII

I do not excuse people who, out of pride,
Deny the Lord; but the guilt of harmless
And mistaken people seems to me much less:
They deny a God who does not exist —
One who, despite omnipotence, does not prevent evil.

Evil in the world is not willed
By a Power that acts as if It were sleeping;
It is in the nature of All-Possibility,
Beyond the personal God, in the Depth of the Essence —

But not as evil; as a tribute to Becoming —
For far from God is all being on earth.
The benevolent God is near — be not afraid;
In all existence, the Lord is concealed.

CXXIV

Harp and flute — then male and female voices:
Fountains of sound that bear witness
To the soul and to beatitude;
The golden waves of Heaven and of the Spirit —

Like angels, adorning the Gardens of the Praised One:
Coming from within and leading within.

CXXV

David was not only king and prophet,
He was also poet, harpist and singer —
He danced in ecstasy before the Ark,
As it is written in the Bible.

"The Lord is my Shepherd, I shall not want."
A prophet's words, and a liberating prayer.

CXXVI

The feet of the dancer: they move inwards,
Yet they stand motionless at the center —
Then her hands: *mudrās* which teach,
And which honor the inward by exteriorization;

The body: it praises the Lord in its own way —
Chalices of beauty that constantly return;
Thus does the earth revolve as it moves round the sun.

CXXVII

Man can speak, and so make the inward audible;
He can sing, and so give life to the soul's music;
He can also whisper, and so veil secrets;
And he can cry out, when threatened by the world —

Let him cry to God in the trials of existence.
If ye understand well the meaning of things:
The first cry of a child is a prayer;

So also is the last rattle before death —
God grant that man inherit the voice of the angels.

But this voice lies not only in a distant becoming —
Calling upon God, ye possess it already on earth.

CXXVIII

Thou grievest over injustice which,
Out of foolishness, they committed against thee;
Go thou on, do not look back —
Wisdom means waiting.

The meaning of life lies before thy gaze,
A garden of hope;
Think of the highest goods that await thy heart
In the presence of God.

CXXIX

It is man's deepest substance
That draws him toward God:
Often it is the "I": individual feeling, faith or wish;
With others, it is the self-forgetting vision of the Intellect,
Directed towards Ipseity.

But all men are equal as men —
On their way to the Kingdom of Heaven.

CXXX

Where there is light, there must also be shadow.
Certainly, evil is no absolute;
But light must fight against darkness —
Remember: *Adveniat regnum tuum.*

Songs without Names

Fourth Collection

At every moment thou canst find refuge in God;
God hears the soul that speaks in secret.
The Lord is always ready to receive —
Thou must be ready; the door is never closed.

Songs without Names

Fourth Collection

I

In God's Presence: no object
From outside, no sound from within the soul —
No thou, no I. Truth and the Name;
This in the eternal Now — be it thus thy whole life long.

II

God-remembrance must change man,
For the purpose of a lamp is to give light;
If our soul is not improved,
Then reciting pious formulas is of no avail.

Renounce false greatness — become small
And selfless, and thou wilt be in Heaven.

III

Look to the future, not to false hopes;
Earthly things come to thee of themselves.
For thee, the future should be spiritual realization,
And not an idle dream of earthly desires.
So know that the true future is
What thou art in thy deepest being.

IV

"The heart of the wise is in the house of mourning,"
Said Solomon. This is so because the sage
Has no true home in the world of dreams —
The wise man's heart is always journeying,

And yet is motionless, true to its Center.
It is the world of dreams that passes by his heart.

V

"The heart of the fool is in the house of joy,"
Said Solomon. For in the fool's dream
Sensual pleasure is the sole purpose of life —
Duty is nothing for him, he lives in empty foam.

The good man also knows of earthly pleasure,
On the basis of the duty that he must fulfill;
Towards men, within the realm of time —
And especially with a view to golden Eternity.

VI

Dignity and self-domination have disappeared
From our world. I praise the animals —
They have remained true to themselves. Only man
Has pushed his behavior into nothingness.

Letting oneself go — one should not tolerate it;
Blessèd is he who can say "no" to his soul.
Dignity is somehow the natural garment of man —
Is he not made in the image of the Creator?

VII

There have been mystics who behaved badly —
Because they wanted people to mock them.
It is similar, and yet different, in our time —
People want to make ridiculous whatever is noble.

A remark: humility is false
If it is not concerned with the well-being of others.
Truth, says Plato, involves the radiation of the beautiful —
You should not rob your neighbor of this right.

VIII

Such is the world — worries and sorrows;
All to no avail.
Thou hast the choice; be wise, and choose
The happiness of Being.

Repose in what thou essentially art,
Beyond this earth,
So that the to-and-fro of useless thinking
May become contemplation.

IX

When one is not directly engaged in prayer —
What should one do?
Work that is necessary and meaningful —
One cannot simply rest

In this world. An inner instinct tells me
That I must write
And teach. How else could I
Occupy my time?

X

What the spirit and the heart teach us
Is independent of whatever we may hear.
Stubbornness should never be praised —
For knowledge comes from Above.

XI

One may call good, from a pious point of view,
What the rules demand;
One must call good what bears witness to the Most High,
What every man must understand as virtue —

What lies in the nature of things — not in appearance.
The absolute bears witness to pure Being.

XII

The problem of exaggeration: a learned man
Told me that God never demands,
Through the law, what is unreasonable;
Moderation in everything is the wise man's adornment.

A saint may well be unreasonable —
But this behavior is for him alone.

XIII

The ego is proof of the Supreme Self;
The thing is proof of the Creator of all things,
Pure Being. Whoever does not see this,
No miracle on earth can make wiser.

XIV

The soul should base itself on thoughts
That are useful to its meaning and destiny;
It should not flutter in the realm of dreams,
Only to arrive at a vain illusion.
Understand, O man, what is real and divine,
And become what thou art in the Divinity.

XV

In my youth, I often heard
That Germans are bad, and they alone.
I must be what I am, and what God wills;
For what reason should I be different?
And moreover: I know that no entire people is bad;
And what the world is, I know now better than ever.

XVI

Certainly the warrior's profession must exist,
Otherwise it would be impossible to live in the *kali-yuga*.
In the golden age, there was no bloodshed;
But our time is iron, blood must flow —
Be that as it may, I must add one thing:
Warriors are heroes, but nevertheless they are killers.

XVII

Certainly nomadic people must hunt —
Otherwise they would find nothing to fill their stomachs.
People say that bullfighting is cruel, and with reason —
But hunting with beaters is no better than bullfighting.
The deer too must be unhappy —
Hunters are holy only in appearance.

XVIII

Man has a brain in order to think;
And he has a mouth in order to speak the truth.
Man is made to manifest God;
Only prayer brings him to God.

God thought — and thus was born the circle of existence;
God spoke — He spoke what the depth of the heart knows.

XIX

One would like to soar on high,
In the light, but one must also live with small things,
Where the earnest is combined with jest —
Everyday things flow into the realm of greatness,
And everything finds its right level.

XX

Sadness of soul is a ploy of the evil one —
The first response should be indifference
To everything that is not the Highest Truth.

The second response is resignation;
The third is a joyous "yes,"
Faith in the Lord's compassion —

Hope and gratitude, where thou art.

XXI

In old age, one has many memories —
One wonders where one's home may be.
The past — many beautiful experiences have faded away;
I think of happiness by the green Rhine.

In Mostaghanem I spent golden days
By the sea, with palm trees and shimmering mosques;
Here my heart was placed on God's scales.

Then the wheel of destiny turned:
And saw me near the world of the Alps —
Here many important inspirations came to me.

Where is the homeland? It is not a place —
The heart is thy home. It is where
Heaven bestows on us its ultimate Mercy.

XXII

In my early youth, my salvation was
Shri Shankara, and with him, spiritual virtue;
And so I was able to learn: only inspiration,
And not vain thinking, can give Wisdom.
Then came the notion of tradition:
Only the sacred may carry the sacred.

All this Guénon wrote in his works with great diligence
And zeal. But much still remained to be said!

XXIII

First, Shri Shankara — he is the greatest;
Then Ramanuja, who taught about the Creator.
Then Lallā, who exteriorized the Self,
And who, dancing for the Godhead, made herself naked;
Also Abhinavagupta, who converted
Earthly pleasure into spirituality.
This completes the circle, created by the *Sanātana Dharma* —
A circle that delivers men from the world.

XXIV

In India it is said that wise men know God;
But it is also said that He is unknown to the wise.
The viewpoints are different; the question is
What, in the wise man's mind, is called God.
Not everything in the Godhead can be expressed
In words — one should leave in peace
What goes beyond speech and reason.

XXV

Every day, the Sufi has three thoughts:
Consciousness of his imperfection;
Consciousness of what he should be;
And consciousness of Divine Infinity.

First: may Allah forgive me;
Then: may the Prophet dwell in my heart;
And then: there is but One Reality —
And this will reward the believer with God.

XXVI

The chief reason to think of God
Is because there is nothing higher than He.
And may God so guide my steps,
That He may love me.

XXVII

A guiding thought comes to my mind:
That fundamentally I am God-remembrance.
It is my heart that reckons thus —
Because, in its inmost depth, it is what is.

XXVIII

To most people, it seems obvious
That our world is just as it looks;
In the superstition of this picture book,
Almost everyone is firmly united

And they do not ask why there is I-consciousness —
Why everyone is simultaneously
An I and a thou. In the face of this enigma,
The average man just closes his eyes.

XXIX

The dignity of a noble man is not superficial;
It is based on a profound reality:
The immovable Center amidst the circling
Of the world; the wheel of existence is consecrated to God.

As Aristotle taught: silent
Is the cause of all things. Nobility
Is participation in Pure Being;
This lies deep in the blood of the noble man.

The principle of dignity should resound in the heart —
Dignity means:
               to bring Being into our existence.

XXX

Country and history — deceiving hells;
Both are dream-veils that lead to nothing;
You cannot gain anything in dreams —
In veils you can only lose yourselves.

It is true that the ephemeral manifests eternal values;
But images are made to fade away.
Only beyond all dreams, in the inmost heart,
Can you attain to Truth and to yourselves.

XXXI

Things, which may or may not be —
This is the chain of which life is made;
God is what must be, He is Necessity.
Life ends in the night of death —

Because it was not Being. It was only possibility,
Like a flower that will fade,
And only for a time decorates the meadow.

And yet: there is the golden farness of Eternity;
Thy heart lives — a star among a thousand stars.

XXXII

In Nature, and also in man, there are
Appearances of beauty and of strength;
Whoever experiences these, should not tend to the outward.
He should be fascinated by God's work —

He must, with new wings, live towards the inward —
And find in the depths of his own heart
What the symbols of the sensorial world proclaim.

XXXIII

Profundity and strength, richness and joy of life
With a little melancholy and a warlike mentality —
Thus ride Russia's singers, like a storm
Over the boundless steppes.

Many a one pours out his heart in burning songs —
May the Lord answer the ardor of the soul.

XXXIV

Spanish melodies, falling from the lute like pearls —
Enchantment and love in Andalusian nights;
It seems to me as if these songs of longing
Bring me greetings from the Macarena.

Longing and love are in each song —
And also fulfillment and the peace that comes from faith.

XXXV

It might be asked why it is permissible for me
To mention small things alongside the great;
Firstly, because what is small is often useful;
Secondly, because small things are dependent on the great;

And finally, because one should see the small in relation
To the great Truth. The great radiates
Even through the smallest. Everything in the world
Is well-protected in the womb of Divinity.

XXXVI

To see the Lord in everything means:
Thou knowest that every noble thing is proof of the Most High;
To see everything in the Most High means:
That everywhere thou bowest down before the Divinity.

Be thou in God — by thinking of Him;
He will be in thee, because thou gavest thyself to Him.

XXXVII

Upward: the way to Heaven
                    and the Most High;
Downward: the way to wrath
                    and the fire of the judgement.
Forward: the way to the future
                    and the goal;
Backward: the way to the past
                    and to nothingness.
To the right: the way to serious choice,
                    to activity;
To the left: the enjoyment of the good —
                    peace, repose.

Outward: thou wilt endlessly
                    dissipate thyself;
Inward: thou wilt take joy
                    in the One.

XXXVIII

The anticipation — within the proof itself —
Of the thesis one wishes to prove,
Is false thinking; but not so the axiom,
Which is truth, and is despised only by the fool.

True is what testifies to the nature of things,
Even if one keeps silent regarding the line of reasoning.

XXXIX

In mid-life, the fan is open:
One sees before oneself so many possibilities;
In old age, the fan is soon to close:
One must prepare oneself for the end —

But duration should not wear us down,
For God is God; the world remains the world —
We are what we have been since the beginning:
The capacity to love the Highest Good.

XL

Devotion and fervor are the two doors
To God-remembrance: the soul should be motionless
In meditation, and glowing with life
In the God-consecrated cavern of the heart.

The urge of the spirit is for height and depth:
Holy silence, innermost song.

XLI

One God and He alone; then the Prophets
And the Books; creation and the end of the world.
Man and immortality —
There is nothing there that the Spirit cannot find worthy of faith.

What attracts thee to God? Perhaps a myth —
A dramatic, overwhelming event;
Or else the archetype of all religion,
Which the pneumatic finds in his heart.

XLII

It is strange how small things can give us joy —
Why? Because, after thinking, they give us rest;
And then: because it moves us deeply
That Heaven should wish to give us even the smallest of things.

XLIII

In pious old songbooks I used to find
So much lamentation over our life
And death; is there nothing else in existence
But misery?
Ye believe in God, yet are close to despair —
If only ye knew: your most beautiful dream,
Ye have it already in prayer —

                              for God is here!

XLIV

In all sectors of humanity, there are limits
That are typological. Religion
Must take account of this, for it is the garment of Truth;
Naked Truth is the reward of the wise.

XLV

"All is vanity," said Solomon.
But I would say that the world is indifferent
With regard to the True, whose kernel
We bear in the depths of our heart.

The wind blows away all earthly vanity,
Be joyous in God. *Shalōm, Salām.*

XLVI

Selfishness and vengefulness, and therefore pettiness,
These are incompatible with the contemplation of God;
It is not that one should never punish evil —
But before the Lord thou shouldst not harbor bitter thoughts.

Many a one who grew up under the rule of wicked people
May bear within himself much anger,
As a self-defense; because the world
Sought to murder his soul from early on.

Not wickedness, but weakness,
Noble people will forgive.
                    Peace is the Godhead's very Being.

XLVII

Strong is not the one who has banished compassion;
The strongest of men are not monsters —
Strong are those to whom magnanimity is dear,
Like Saladin, whom Dante acknowledged.

A drop of gentleness lies in the hero's blood,
And strength benefits the noble woman.
And so everywhere: gentleness lies in the rigorous —
The rigorous may be tinged with gentleness.

A word of the Lord: verily, my Mercy
Precedeth my Wrath, and waiteth for the poor.

XLVIII

Brahmin, kshatriya — the difference
Is not absolute. The nature
Of the spiritual is unity: each pole
Contains the other, even if only a little.
Priest and warrior, saint and hero
Are opposites — but nevertheless constitute one world.

Love and anger are in the hero's nature —
But thou canst also find them in sacerdotal souls;
The thinking and the contemplativity of the sacerdotal man —
Thou seest them also in the hero's holiness.
Yin-Yang: in a word, the sacerdotal
Contains, and permeates, the royal.

XLIX

Unitive thought and separative thought:
Synthesis, analysis. But the latter
Should never predominate; look not,
With astonished gaze, upon the flowering meadow
Of phenomena. For the emphasis must be
On the One, and not on analysis.

The sage looks above all at the Center —
To be one with the Center is his heart's desire.

L

Be happy because God is Truth and Peace;
Because one must be resigned to God's Will;
Because He never forgets the misery of man.

The Eternal is the Highest Good;
The soul cannot aspire to anything better
Than That whereon its true being is founded.

Trials are necessary. Has God forgotten you?
The limits of the trial, ye cannot measure.
And what ye are, is what ye do in God.

LI

Freedom — but within the framework of our duty:
Man is free in proportion to the height of his spirit;
He who knows not himself, deserves not freedom.

Libertas — but not in the form of arbitrariness:
Freedom is not made in order to reach the point
Where nobility no longer exists in the world.

Freedom does not mean: the right of vain louts
In the end, to abolish every freedom —
And may God grant that we understand what is right.

LII

If one wants to assess the rebelliousness of the people,
One should not forget the stupidity of the nobles:
Tradition is fine and good —
But decadence provokes the people's wrath.
One sees it in the incredible costumes
That made the nobles' feasts ridiculous —
Who dominated himself for the sake of the people?
And unfortunately, the Church gave its blessing to all this.

LIII

Understand that within love dwell beauty
And greatness — something of the melody
Of the Eternal. A man may be nothing much,
Just an anybody — but love is never small.

A man who once was redeemed by love —
Has once in his life been great.
When love moves deeply into thy heart —
Be happy that it blooms for the Divinity.

LIV

The voice of the folk-song bears witness to olden times,
And also to many things from later days —
To springtime joy and heart-felt sorrow;
To all that people carry in their souls.

And then there is the luminous dignity of church hymns —
They remove many burdens from the heart.
Vox populi, vox Dei — this means:
God grant that the bell may ring within yourselves.

LV

Gypsy violinists, bards and minstrels,
Leading a homeless, wandering life:
A beautiful vocation, if consecrated to God —
Gaining much, and losing nothing,
For beauty has its end in God's Truth;
It is the vocation of the priest, who preaches —
It is a holy play adorning a human life.

LVI

Mental images can be like houses
In which we dwell. Some are good;
Others are not. If one of them please thee not:
Why enclose thyself within its darkness —

Within an emptiness, that tells thee nothing about God?

LVII

Good behavior is not for others —
It is for God, and also to teach ourselves.
Do not say to thyself: I was alone;
For one owes oneself a flawless behavior
Even if one were in the midst of the desert.

LVIII

Many are of the opinion that an idea is nothing,
And that what counts is pure concentration;
Being, not thinking. But I say, on the contrary,
The idea is everything, mere being is illusion.

It is from the idea that is fashioned the being of the heart:
What I think, I become. Every child knows
That the graces of realization are already contained
In the idea of Eternity.

LIX

And many believe that thinking is enough —
Such as philosophers, who live from books,
And think that their brain is divine.
Fruitless conjecture is their vain effort —

These are but phantasms that the wind of time will blow away.
And that is why we stand where we stand today.

LX

Only an empty head can be bored —
Only he who knows not boredom is truly human.
For to be human is to be a mirror that receives
Light from God; man is none other than this.

LXI

According to Plato, knowledge is recollection.
Artificial pseudo-wisdom comes from the devil,
Even if the theory glitters — *se non è vero,*
E ben trovato — of this there is no doubt.

Ye wish to obtain light from your nothingness?
Truth comes from above and from within!

LXII

The golden robe of Truth has two sides:
One-and-Onliness and Selfhood —
Pure Being and Self. But, so that no scission should appear,
I tell thee that the two sides are the Great One.

LXIII

"Give us," said Jesus, "our daily bread":
The bread of the Spirit. For ultimately
Only the man whose actions strive toward God's intention,
Has a right to life.

LXIV

Fools think that in Heaven,
Everything we had on earth is lost;
They know not that the beauty of this life
Is in the Most High — and also, through God, within thyself.

LXV

The world is like the vast starry space,
And like the ocean — one can scarcely count so many things.
So much has remained unknown to me —
But if I knew it, I would love it totally.

LXVI

The *Bhakti-Avatāras* possess crowns,
In the midst of which they dwell like pearls.
Krishna in Vrindavan — his radiant garland
Was the drunken dance of the naked *gopis*.

Such is Light: a felicity radiated outwards —
Which, in gratitude, flows back to its Source.

LXVII

The mild summer night descended upon me —
An inner voice spoke: dream gently
Of light and love — thy heart will
Awaken to the One Light and to its Self.

LXVIII

Spiritual contemplation, *darshan*, means nourishing ourselves
From the thing we look at, and venerating its form —
Blossoming through its presence;
Not only the soul, but also the limbs of the Guru
Are sacred; they bring down a grace,
And radiate outwards from the Spirit's might.
Also the voice of the sage, which we hear,
Will turn us to our better self —
Whoever has ears to hear, let him keep watch.

LXIX

"The Spirit is willing, but the flesh is weak":
I am not thinking here of the moral aspect,
But only of the fragility of man;
This follows man in every situation —
Not only the weak, but also the faithful.

The Lord will pardon for the sake of the good intention —
Sincerity is gold on the scales of God.

LXX

Co-operation, and yet opposition,
Between work and faith — act and fervor:
Two paths given us by the Sovereign Good,
Liberating the soul from the tyranny of ignorance —

Praise be to God, that in the seed here-below
Something of the harvest is already granted.

LXXI

The Highest Word is not hair-splitting —
Rather, it is dignity, and also music;
It is as if, in a summer night,
We were brought love and wisdom's wine.

The Highest Word resounds in the earthly world
Just as one tells ancient tales to children —
And just as if the light of divine Wisdom
Were a poem streaming from the heart.

LXXII

Do not believe that Shri Shankara was God —
He was a man. He sought to convince us
That two and two are four; and that on every
Point, we should bow down before his logic.

Meanwhile the goddess, who sent him to teach,
Proved *Brahma satyam* through her dancing.

LXXIII

The dance of the goddess is the manifestation
Of Pure Being in all existential forms;
Dance is a proof, because Beauty is Truth,
Beyond the world of mental criteria —

Beyond the language of dialectic.
But there must also be the language of things themselves —
Symbols can form our souls.

And let the Godhead weave knowledge.

LXXIV

Is not *Samprasāda* the highest good?
It is serene soaring above all things —
It is the Benares that we ourselves are.
The truth of *Ātmā* gives wings to the soul.

LXXV

There is a difference between Reality and appearance;
And another between thinking and being.
Certainly, thou canst find an explanation for the world;
But what thou art — thou canst not comprehend it.

LXXVI

A proverb says: it is too beautiful to be true;
But Plato says: beauty is the splendor of the Truth.
The popular refers to transience —
The people do not fully grasp the nature of beauty.

The essence of the beautiful blooms beyond time:
Only the sign of beauty can be transient.
Understand that the love-songs of this world
Reach deep into the essence of the Ideas.

LXXVII

God-consciousness — hast thou really understood
That it gives peace to the one who grasps it?
Man's happiness lies not only in possession —
The pious man is happy because he loves.

The sign that love of God is sincere,
Is that thou art happy.

LXXVIII

Guru is Brahma — says a sacred adage
In the land of the Ganges. But it is also well known
That guru is *Māyā*; both are true.
Understand that Brahma becomes *Māyā*;
Nevertheless unites in the luminous sound of *Om*.

LXXIX

It might be asked whether we have a right
To the enjoyments that life offers —
Should one not make penance, is not sacrifice
Required in a world where folly rages?

Certainly, there must be renunciation and sobriety —
But also respect for the deep dignity
Of Beauty, for it bestows the wine of the Spirit.
In what is noble there is also pleasure, not merely burden;
There is also an opening towards the Above.
                                        People are not
All alike, nor are the paths to the Kingdom of Heaven.

LXXX

Principle and manifestation; one could also say:
God and the world. After this, come space and time,
Matter and energy, subject and object,
Cause and effect. God's ways are vast.

Container and content form the web
From which all existence is made;
Then form and number. Thus hath the Lord
Brought forth the possible from nothingness to light.

One could enumerate many other pairs;
I had to choose just seven out of many —
And praise be to God, Who conceived this interweaving.

LXXXI

The ascetic seeks not only to obtain salvation —
He also seeks to escape the grief
Caused by earthly attachment,
The grief caused when the Eternal sings within the ephemeral.

Earthly harmony — a path to God —
But it is also not without sorrow.

LXXXII

A great commentary on the Brahma-Sutra —
Simpler than this, it seems to me, is what is crystal clear:
That Brahma is true, that the world of *Māyā* is but appearance;
That our soul contains the light of Brahma.

First, the idea; then concentration on the True —
And may God keep us in His Mercy!

LXXXIII

Remembrance of God knows no number —
A single time is many thousand times,
And conversely. If thou wilt pronounce the Name of the Most High —
Thou must carry it throughout thine entire life.

What for God is one — and for Him alone —
Must be, for time-bound people, without end.

LXXXIV

First *certitudo*, then *serenitas* —
How often should thy soul remember these!
Serenity is to walk above the clouds —
Certitude of God comes from the inmost depths.

The great weakness is forgetfulness —
Man lets himself be seduced by time.
Sadness is to measure with false measures;
Despair is to forget the light of certitude.

The spiritual image of man is like a tree:
The root grows, and high above space blooms.

LXXXV

Serenity is Divine Nature;
It is joy, that adorns the world with blossoms;
Then love, that brings forth the fruits of existence;
Then longing that leads the world into autumn.

Our soul is made in the image of God;
Hear, O heart, what resounds in thy depths.
For in thee dwells He to whom praise is due —

Be thou the harpist, who extols Being.

LXXXVI

In India it was the custom among the brahmins
To meet for debate,
And to dispute for hours over *Advaita*,
Until one among them was victor.

One can argue endlessly about ideas,
But finally the flow of thoughts must cease;
And, like lightning, That which is shines forth —

And, along with Being, the Self that thou art.

LXXXVII

Theodicy — it is a two-edged sword, because in it
Being is equated with Beyond-Being;
Being — the Personal God — does not wish evil;
All-Possibility alone is the cause of evil.

The good in the wide world proves
That the substance of the Godhead is the Good;
Evil is only a brief cycle,
Whose kernel rests in the womb of possibilities.

And what God cannot exclude,
He can only prevent in part;
We cannot dictate to the Heavenly Powers
What they must do and not do.

LXXXVIII

In principle, every man can become a saint,
Otherwise he would not be a human being.
In fact, only he can become a saint whose ego
Has received the grace that God ordained for him.

Almost everyone can experience wonderful graces —
But only the noble man can ascend to the Most High;

Noble is not he who has no weakness —
Noble is he who has no vice.

All are human beings, but few are called —
The substance of a man has degrees;

Man has capacities and instincts —
But what is decisive, is the love of God.

LXXXIX

Bad character is responsible for itself,
Even if there has been a trauma. But different is
The case of a trauma one is not responsible for —
So be just when measuring souls.
An injustice can deeply wound a noble person —
But his core remains gold, and you must acknowledge it to him.

XC

We distinguish between a place and Infinity;
And likewise between an event and Eternity.

These are the two compelling ideas;
Through them, neither world nor time can endure.

O Eternity, in which time crystallizes —
O Infinity, which extends toward the inward.

Ye men, who have always been beggars —
God has made beautiful for you the seriousness of existence.

XCI

A child who has been burned — says a proverb —
Is afraid of fire; by this one means that
What one expects is something dark.
But one could also see the saying in a brighter light,
Because a child, who has received a gift, looks forward to a feast;

Patience and trust in God are the best.

XCII

In a time when our world was still dreaming —
When there were still fairies, mermaids and dragons,
Mountain spirits, salamanders and the like —

There were also many miraculous signs.
But today's gray world is like a tomb:
Cold reason has taken away its soul.

The heavenly powers have withdrawn;
The evil one has emptied hearts;
With his lies, he has turned the world to ice.

Only a few are the heirs of better times —
But whether late or early, whatever bears witness to God cannot die.

XCIII

What is valid for the macrocosm,
Is also valid for the microcosm — thy soul.
The Golden Age slumbers within thee —
God grant that thy heart may choose the Good.

The world is not free, it is only a symbol —
But man is free by virtue of his divine nature.

XCIV

Ye think of times when miracles occurred;
Today one wishes to deprive the world of meaning,
And unbelief wants to destroy the sacred —
Patience. The divine rod of Moses is waiting.

Striking the rock, he drew forth living water —
A symbol of what the Spirit brings about
When a fateful hour has struck —
Light, which man carries deep within.

XCV

I call it exteriorization with a view to interiorization.
When our senses look outwards
A renewed ardor is aroused within us —
The outward propels us inwards.

Similar — but not exactly the same — is this: it is not the outward
That causes us, through grace, to turn towards the inward:
It is spiritual intention that comes first —
This gains for us the grace of ecstasy.

Drunkenness of spirit deeply penetrated
King David's heart as he danced before the pious people,
Before the liberated shrine in the Holy Land —
And before Michal, his wife, who understood nothing.

XCVI

Blind obedience and nobility of soul
Are not the same. Hold high
The banners of the law; but in a blameless soul,
Thou canst sense the fragrance of Paradise.

Many have carried obedience to extremes —
Few there are who love because they love.

XCVII

The imperfection of things,
Their ephemerality, cannot but sadden our heart.

But their perfume of eternity and infinity
Cannot but give joy to those who love the True.

One goes to sleep with the troubles of the gray day;
Then comes the long night — what will the morrow bring?

Once I heard a voice as I awoke:
Be still — let not thyself be troubled.

XCVIII

The world is made of contradictions —
Hast thou not yet seen through the play of existence?
Thou knowest the opposites: pleasure and pain;
But one does not always have the choice between the two.
Thou see'st the dark and thou see'st the light,
But thou also see'st the essential — so choose
Whatever builds for thee a bridge to the Real.

XCIX

The radiant green of meadows, bushes, trees —
This is the earthly realm that God has given us;
Flowers, blossoms, birdsong;
Everywhere home, and a life that finds happiness in existence.

All this occurred to me; and I can think of much more.
It falls to me to offer the Lord a loving heart.

C

Certitude of God calls for nobility of soul,
And also brings the consolation of certitude of salvation.
Certitude of salvation calls for fear of God
And good works. The Most High is angry
With those who handle Truth too lightly,
And seek not to know His holy Will.

In this world certitude, and nobility of soul,
Are the defense against the army of illusion.
Certitude of God is unconditional;
But the presentiment of salvation is a grace that beckons from afar.

CI

To receive is good, if it is not egoism —
If thou put a giving into thy receiving;
If people grasp what thou art in the Lord —
If thy joy be founded on the love of God.

CII

Saintly people often have to suffer
Because of the evil one. Ye must know:
Where there is a great light, there must also be shadows —
Sanctity is certainly not a cushion to rest on.

It can also happen that one suffers for others;
The suffering of a saint is not his fault.
He allows the world to be what its nature will;
His consolation is certitude — and patience.

Thou may'st wonder about a scoundrel —
But never about a trial from the Most High.

CIII

You must understand the troubadours aright —
They sought to see the Divine in woman;
Quite other was the attitude of the ascetical and rigorous —
They sought to die before dying.

All wished to find Wisdom and Unity —
All wished to link life with death.

CIV

And when ye pray, use not many words,
Said Jesus, for this the heathens do;
They think that Heaven will listen to them,
If they persevere in their long discourses.

One cannot remember this too much:
If ye have profound faith, it suffices
That ye think inwardly on the Divine Name.

CV

When Christ spoke against long prayers,
He was thinking of petitions, not of God's words,
Which penetrate us and fill us with light:
For example, David's psalms, which are like the Gate of Heaven —

Words that not only speak of God,
But also express the petitions of men.

CVI

What does epistemology seek to explain?
The nature of consciousness and of knowing;
Then the content of consciousness, its objects;
And then the art of discernment and of definition.

There are five modes of understanding:
Firstly sense-perception on the material plane;
Then the instinctive knowledge of all living creatures;
Then reason, which perceives rules and laws.

Then spiritual knowledge, regarding God and the world —
And also regarding final things, their why and how.
And finally I must mention prophecy —
Which delivers the Divine discourse to the world.

CVII

There are seekers who know too much,
But understand nothing; their mind is as if torn;
With others, one need but say one thing —
And they understand everything, because they know how to think.

Do not think this excessive or exaggerated —
It is written in the substance of the Spirit.
Thou need'st not be extremely clever —
Thou may'st nevertheless enjoy the Truth!

CVIII

Reason alone — you see where it leads;
We would have done better to remain with a myth —
With a divine dream, and hence with the Pure Spirit;
With the right to live, and the right to love.

CIX

Joy in multiplicity and joy in unity —
On the one hand, the meadow of flowers and the shimmering
Sea of stars; on the other hand, the one and only sun —
And the Spirit in the depths of thy being.

Creation — no one can find its limits;
Praise be to the Self that none can fathom.

CX

The soul must grow accustomed to God's grace —
For man cannot easily bear peace.
He lacks patience and gratitude —
He should rejoice, but he likes to complain.

CXI

Man wants life and he flees the naught;
He seeks whatever will pass the empty time for him.
Emptiness should not cause him grief —
For nothing is nothing. God is what always remains.

CXII

David danced before the Ark of the Covenant;
Around Krishna danced the garland of loving *gopis*.
The universe is made of nothing and of joy —
There is no other choice but death and dance.

And Lallā, when she found the deepest Self,
Transcended form, and danced naked on the rim of existence.

CXIII

"In old age, everything fades away, but God comes,"
A storyteller wrote. One thing is certain:
The coming of God. But the question remains,
Whether or not our weak heart has withdrawn from the world.

CXIV

Who is greater: the one who is perfectly holy,
Or the one who is perfectly wise? These two
Greatnesses clasp hands; far be it from us
To compare one kind of gold with another.

Truth is everything; thou canst not reach it
Without the golden light of beauty of soul.

CXV

In my childhood, I was told that
Nature had chosen naïvety for me,
Because I firmly believed that one and one are two,
And did not believe that a cat is a bird.

If one wants to drink from the fountain of Wisdom —
One must have the necessary gifts.

CXVI

How can people, who dwell in a God-given peace,
Combat the absurdity
That this world stupidly creates,
And at the same time not succumb to outward agitation?

They can do so because the peace is God-given,
And because the heart of him who acts is full of light
And quiet — and so the Truth may conquer.

CXVII

Man is made not only of proud power
And wise nature, but also of weakness.
In thinking and in acting, there are dangers
He must know. He should walk the paths
That reveal God's light and nearness,
And should pray that Heaven help him!

CXVIII

Eppur si muove — is it true that the Earth
Really moves? That is the question.
But if you really knew what the issue was,
You would spare yourselves the trouble of asking questions.

Ma già volgeva il mio disio e il velle
L'Amor che muove il sole e l'altre stelle.

CXIX

What was the cloud in which Enoch was raised
To Heaven, when the Lord took him to Himself?
What was the silver cloud, in which Moses,
Elias and Jesus went to Heaven?

The chariot was an unearthly ray —
No one has described from what this cloud was made.
It carried, while she was yet on earth, the body of the Blessed Virgin
From the Holy Land to Spain, to the *pilar.*

And in the same chariot the Prophet was conveyed
From the desert sands to the Holy City.

CXX

Noble mentality and correct behavior
Are God-remembrance; not in themselves,
But joined with the act of Remembrance;
The desire of the heart faithfully to manifest God-consciousness.

Whoever is ugly in his very substance,
Whatever be his works, forgets the Lord.
Not only actions count, but also being, in stillness.
Jesus called this: his Father's Will.

CXXI

Beyond-Being, Being, Existence:
This encompasses the entire doctrine of Reality.
If we compare Beyond-Being to space,
Then It would have our sun as companion.

The moon is analogous to Existence; without the sun's light,
The silvery image of the moon does not exist.
Where then dost thou place the earth?
The earth is the human intellect, which sees.

CXXII

The ball of the sun is a real symbol;
An artificial symbol can be anything.
A true symbol is a proof
Of Reality, in the midst of dream, illusion, and appearance.

But a proof is not the thing in itself;
You must not mistake the sun for the True.
But one may pray to the True through the image —
It may be that the Heavenly powers will hear.

CXXIV

Mighty is the pulse-beat of the Godhead,
Or the Godhead's breathing — Brahma's days and nights;
Thou wishest that every day of God
Would bring thee thy same tiny ego's dream;

Be not concerned over thine earthly trivialities —
Be happy that a ray of Truth has come.

CXXV

In earthly things there is always ephemerality —
But love is outside time.
The worldly man understands not what love is;
That in it lies the fragrance of Eternity.

CXXVI

The Bible says: In the beginning was the Word.
A poet wrote: In the beginning was the Act.
The Word is synonymous with Pure Being;
For out of Being comes the seed of all things.

Ye may ask what is at the end —
Look at the mysterious wheel of life.
If ye ask me what beatitude is —
At the beginning is the path of the love of God.

CXXVII

San Juan de la Cruz warned us
About false conviction, which the devil
Casts into souls in order to destroy peace —
Better than false sureness is doubt.

If all too great a grace is given you,
Then the evil one seeks to weave a shadow into it.

CXXVIII

The substance of the saint is nobility
And humility; he cannot be abnormal.
Baseness, pride, and perversity are alien to him;
He is free from all grave defects.

Some saints are so made,
That they only take from God;
Others, such as prophets, are so made that they give —
They give sight to those who previously were blind.

But the saint who receives
Also gives something — through his presence.

And the one who gives, receives before giving —
Because before God, every man is a petitioner.

Sanctity means to be linked
To God — a link of a particular kind,
Depending on the nature of the man, for the world is vast.

And God chose you before ye existed.

CXXIX

Rapture or ecstasy: it may differ
According to the spiritual space in which it blossoms.
One man is pulled by the Most High toward Himself;
Another man pulls himself toward the Most High.

With one, ecstasy is a sweet wine —
With another, it is of a more sober nature.

CXXX

Between the earthly man and the Lord,
There is the divine man — a bridge
From nothingness to the All. Chance and Necessity:
The primordial and ideal man fills the gap.

No one can meet God — it has been said —
Who does not first meet His Messenger;
Only he who has greeted the image of God,
Will be blessed by the Supreme Reality.

CXXXI

The Messenger of God is the whole world —
The world is embodied in God's Messenger.
Through him thou see'st Pure Being —
Thou who art Spirit within the bonds of existence.

"Universal man" — this is what Sufis call the Word of God:
Creation — the place of its revelation.

CXXXII

In a world where all faith is disappearing,
God will forgive without measure
Those who are still believers,
Just as an anxious mother forgives her child.

In hard times, there is a good sign:
It will be easy to reach Heaven.

CXXXIII

At the end of time, the Prophet said,
There will be the greatest grace from the Lord.
A believing people will come and,
Like a flock of birds, will soar to Heaven.

Songs without Names

Fifth Collection

I wished to put down my pen
But could not do so, even though I wished.
A better urge overtook me,
And let me know what I should give.

Songs without Names

Fifth Collection

I

Humility and generosity, then patience together
With trust — these are the sine qua non
Of the noble soul; no one can be holy
Unless he adopt these ways.

II

The Lord is my shepherd; I shall not want.
Even were I in the deep night of death —
He is with me. For His Name's sake,
He has brought me to the light of the day, and to the source.

For His Name's sake — the Name which I invoke —
Both when awake and when asleep.

III

If I tell you that humility is everything —
Humility and generosity — you must understand:
Humility is akin to death, it is the snow of the Spirit;
And generosity is to see with the soul of your neighbor.

Then come patience and trust in God —
To look upon everything with the profundity of the heart.

IV

It is related that the Messenger of God
Once fell from his horse in the presence of a group of believers.
When he arose, he said, "Once in life
God humiliates the one whom He has chosen" —

The one "who was a prophet even before Adam."

V

Trials are purifications that come from God —
Because man must renew himself in God,
And so become deeper; Rome was not built
In a day; one must know oneself.

"Hate thy soul," it is said in Scripture;
Thou canst love within thyself only what comes from God.

VI

It can happen that someone prays for something stupid —
And an answer comes, but it comes from the evil one;
For when the Most High gives no answer,
Satan plays his evil game.

Say not: in such a case one has been too easily misled —
For already in the prayer one has lied to oneself.

VII

The devil said: I can do everything,
The greatest miracles you can imagine —
But one thing I cannot do: kneel down,
For it is said that pride is the greatest of all sins.

VIII

The True and the Beautiful are ready
To pull man out of this vale of tears —
Out of a world full of falsehood and ugliness,
Onto a height where graces bloom.

Truth and Beauty bestow light and joy.
Each says: "I came, I saw, I conquered."

IX

The angels are the Godhead's faculties
In Heaven and on earth; rays of power,
That bring everything about, according to God's will,
And thus paint the great picture of the universe.

It is said there is an angel for every soul;
The highest angel stands before the Throne of God.
And every angel radiates a thousandfold —
There is an angel king for every world.

X

Somewhere in the Bible there is mention
Of dark spirits that appear as angels,
In order to mislead saints and pious people;
They deceive only a few out of many.

For all things show their true colors;
Illusion must give way before Knowledge.

XI

It is in God's nature to manifest Himself,
And also, from afar, to return to Himself;
From afar — because manifestation moves away from God;
And so there must be many kinds of spirits —

Both good and evil. Without this weaving,
The whole creation would remain in suspense.

XII

It is natural that the wicked enemy
Should attack the pious man; but it is not natural
That the pious soul should let himself be seduced —
That he should not notice the devil's ruses

And know that this is the way of the tempter,
With all saints and in all ages;
Illusion does not arise from the holy soul —
But from the evil one, who seeks to lead us into evil.

The devil is never well-intentioned —
He always cunningly has something harmful in mind.
Do not say: in this or that point, the devil is right;
Thou needest not his help; he is bad.

XIII

Who is the "I" of the ray of Revelation?
It is the Lord, and none other, who manifests Himself in a religion,
But in the discourse of the saint,
It is an angel, or his noble personality,
Or it is the luminous shrine of the Intellect.
By accident, it can also be satan —
From without, and never from the good within;
Because a pure heart cannot invent falsehood.

XIV

If one cannot know whether an order
Comes from Heaven or from hell,
One is not obliged to follow it; for no man
Will be condemned because of the nightmare of another.

If someone brings a message that is not believable,
It is but "sounding brass and a tinkling cymbal."

XV

Either thou dwellest in a cave
In order to escape the illusion of things,
Or thou see'st the magic tricks of existence,
And observest from within the outward world's play.

Say not that the earthly world is mere seduction,
And that one can only cry to Heaven for help —
If Heaven were not the origin of all beauty,
It could not be so beautiful on earth.

XVI

The feeling of certitude is not always
Proof of truth; it can also be illusion.
Certitude through knowledge is the right thing —
Only in knowledge is our feeling pure.

Imitation of certitude is the ruse
With which the bridge of all evil is built.

XVII

I ask not others what Truth
And God-consciousness are. Likewise: I know
Without asking what certitude is,
And peace of soul — thus the circle is closed.
Whether other people are honest or not —
I wish, with a pure heart, to be devoted to God
And to trust in Him, knowing that whatever comes
Is safe with Him — and with Him alone.

XVIII

It is often difficult to remain in the Eternal,
Because the world-wheel keeps on turning
And thou must witness coming and going,
And see how nothing stands on the Eternal's ground.

Thou wouldst fain despair of thyself —
But thou bearest Eternity within thee.

XIX

God will not ask thee
About what others do; He will only ask thee
About thyself, and whether thine actions were good or bad;
Thou must only bear thine own burden.

And whatever ye do, be it good or deluded,
The Lord will say: "ye have done this unto Me."

XX

Which would be better, one might ask,
That I should exist or that I should not exist?
The wise man tells himself: my existence
Is also a non-existence; where then shall I be?

God alone is Being. Alongside Being there is nothing —
Nothing but the ray of creative Light.

XXI

Why is *Māyā* so lavish,
Squandering a thousand times what seems to be unique,
In words, images, sounds, and the exuberance of bodies —
A stream weeping before the Face of the Eternal.

Māyā, in her ardor, does not squander —
She only reflects what rests in the Eternal One.

XXII

"Man proposes and God disposes," thus goes a saying;
Very often, disposing is God's only language.
Human thoughts can be like the wind;
But not so God's Will. "Vengeance is mine" —

And "Mine is the favor." Ye cannot force God —
Through the Lord alone can your work prosper.

XXIII

Of humility I have often spoken —
I would also like to emphasize the fear of God.
God will not reward with the gold of His favor
The man who is too cheap.

Love always has reverence in mind;
Without fear, there is no love of God.

XXIV

Confucius taught that everything is reason
And magnanimity. First, universal reason
With its nobility; then the State, which is wise
And noble; and then man in his own fashion.

In Islam, this spirit is combined
With a religion of the love of God;
Prayer at God-appointed times —
And the spiritualization of our God-created instincts.

XXV

The Lord is our refuge — there is no
Better Protector. Even if the world should crumble
When its time has expired —
It is said: a mighty fortress is our God.
May the shrine of thy heart be a mighty fortress —
And thy soul be as a rock.

XXVI

One man, one word — think not that human speech
Is of no consequence; for the Lord has sharp hearing;
What one has promised is not blown away —
It is not something that can be regarded as wind.
It may be that thy mind does violence to the truth —
But what thou forgettest — God forgetteth not.

XXVII

Errare est humanum. Thou shouldst not
Be sick with remorse because thou hast been deceived;
For many have blossomed in the Truth
After having momentarily erred,

And have become better than before.
                                    He who
Learns from a trial, reaps a rich harvest.

XXVIII

The world-wheel turns, and mocks thee —
It does not wish that thy heart aspire to peace.
Saw'st thou not Krishna, who stood in the dark,
And the music of his flute mocked illusion?

In the dark, in Vrindavan's sacred grove.
May it be the refuge of thy soul.
For Vrindavan is more than the cosmic wheel —
It is what thou thyself art before all beginning.

XXIX

The warrior on the battlefield must not flee;
Only one flight is honorable for the hero —
The flight towards God. It is the greatest victory of the soul —
Better than all the victories that fade away.

XXX

The *Bhagavad-Gita* — The Song of the Exalted One;
I read it in my childhood.
"The Exalted One spake" — my heart was healed
By the beauty of this one sentence.

XXXI

Christians and Saracens murder each other —
A sad image, since both are believers.
And yet: it is not wholly without meaning —
For they see, but at the same time they are blind.

XXXII

In German, there are names like "Gottfried,"
"Gottlob," "Gotthold," and "Gottlieb;"[1]
In names lies a power of blessing. From olden times
This was the custom of our pious parents.

Thou shouldst mark well the name "Fürchtegott" —
For only with Fear canst thou tend towards Love.

XXXIII

People said that the Red Indians were savages,
Only half men. The opposite was true:
The sacred for them was everywhere —
If only they could have taught this to the white man!

The white man has corrupted colored men —
Among the young, the sacred has died out;

May God grant that the whole world be converted!

XXXIV

I am in my ninetieth year; I have
Lived many years long with my God,
And nonetheless amidst the noise of people —
Between what troubles us and what uplifts us;
And in the end I could remain in deep peace.

The Lord within me wanted to drive away all illusion —
He, who each day, gives new life to the soul.

XXXV

Europe's folk art is one of the best things
That our Western world has to offer;
Any medieval peasant's hut
Puts the pretentious city palace to shame.

In Scandinavia and Russia,
Indeed almost everywhere, there are the most beautiful buildings
Of wood and the most beautiful handicrafts —
The providential heritage of our forefathers.

XXXVI

"Light comes from the East" — this is true,
If one is thinking of India; but do not forget
Pythagoras, Plato, Plotinus: for many —
Both Christians and Semites — they were a light.

And even the modern West is not made
Only of darkness; one can find traits
In Western man that should be respected;
We do not criticize human values.

XXXVII

It would be wrong to think that music
Is noble only if it is of a sacred kind;
Lyrical music also has its value,
Whether dramatic or delicately intimate.

After all, there is a spiritual value too
In the wild violin playing of gypsy bands;
And I would praise many noble folk songs —
Beauty is Truth, and it comes from Above.

XXXVIII

The animal does not know that one day it will die —
Man alone knows that he is destined for death;
He knows it because he is made in God's image;
He alone is prepared for eternity.

The animal is a fragment and does not know itself;
But man knows of the Day of Judgment;
And for this reason, because spiritually he is all,
He knows: only God is real — I am nothing.

XXXIX

What counts in life? It is that thou avoidest
Whatever is harmful, whatever pulls thee downwards.
What else counts? It is that which thou doest —
The things in which God resounds.

What counts is what thou knowest of the Truth,
And then, what in thee proves to be the Highest Self.

XL

Thou canst not always avoid the absurdity of life?
Be wise, and thou wilt be weary of illusion.
Thou sayst thou canst not always do what is the best —
But whatever thou dost, thou canst repose in the One.
And if thou wishest not to have regrets on thy path —
Then know: it is enough to be with God.

XLI

When one has wandered through nearly a century,
One has lived more than one single life
Here below; one is a "we" inside an "I" —
Destiny was able to weave one and all.

One has lived in a fairy-tale world,
Which for others is no longer real nor graspable;
So this play may elude us too — what counts
Is that the heart forget not the Most High.

XLII

Leucippus, Democritus, and other dreamers
Infatuated with world-explanations, believed in atoms;
But their theories about matter
Were nothing more than mental symptoms.

In reality, in the beginning was the Light
Of the Spirit, which radiated into the darkness of existence,
And congealed in remoteness from God;
Matter has no other origin.

XLIII

There is the theory that all things
Are relative; this theory overlooks
The essential power of the Absolute,
Which manifests, not what vacillates, but what is —

What fills all existence, like the ether.
This was the sound thinking of our fathers.

XLIV

The presence of God — this is one thing;
Then consciousness of God — this is another.
First the Divinity, then man;
Know the goal of thine existence, and go thy way!

XLV

Adam and Eve; and then the Fall.
Man had to be born anew —
Endlessly anew, but always the same man;
Essentially, there is but one human being on earth.

Only one, put there in order to contemplate God —
In order to build a path from nothingness to the All.

XLVI

It is not good that Adam be alone,
Said God; but he must always be renewed,
A creature of many forms within the stream of time.

Adam and Eve are one as they stand
Before God. The one, primordial prayer cannot pass away,
For it belongs to Eternity.

XLVII

Reincarnation — for Hindus and Buddhists
This doctrine from the *Manu-Shāstra* is not merely a fable.
But whether one should take the *Shāstra* literally
Or symbolically is another question.

XLVIII

Truth gives the spirit deep peace;
Beauty gives rise to the miracle of loving.
From Heaven comes God's blessing glance —
Therein lies all wisdom and all happiness.

XLIX

Māyā is a greater enigma than *Ātmā*,
Many Hindus say. In other words:
There is only one problem, that of evil;
As if the world had been a failure on the part of the Creator.

A world there must be, thus remoteness from God,
Evil as a principle. And to say principle,
Is to say manifestation: evil as a thing.
It is meaningless to dare to criticize God.

L

Certitude of God and then certitude of salvation;
The second results from the first.
Then serenity: firstly from the certitude of God,
And then from the certitude of salvation. Light and beatitude.

It never does any harm to repeat
Whatever is useful for others and for oneself.

LI

First, discernment, and then concentration.
First discernment between Reality
And illusion; then between good and evil.
The path from nothingness to God's Pure Being.

Then concentration: first on the Real,
And then on the Good. Love God, thy Lord,
With all thy heart; love what He loves.
Salvation has no other guiding star.

LII

Krishna stands in the center. Upon him gaze
The innumerable *gopis*, beautiful and naked,
And each sees the god in her own way —
The same god — they see him a thousand times.

Enigma of egoity. For the ego, in its essence,
Is one-and-only; it is a single vision,
But multiplied a thousandfold. The web of the world,
How then can it subsist? No one can understand it.

No one but God within us — the Being of Selfhood.
Only He is I; the gopis' gaze is but appearance.

LIII

Three times Greece had a particular greatness:
First, in Plato, as a blessing
For an entire sector of the world; through Plato,
Ancient Greece moved minds profoundly.

Then, in the time of Pericles, began
The false glittering — of Anaxagoras,
And Phidias in the realm of art — a titanesque illusion,
Through which worldliness gained power.

And then: the blessing brought by the Church —
Palamas and Mount Athos, the mysticism
Of the Hesychasts, and the Byzantine empire —
A miracle, watched over by the Turks.

How curious that Islam, which knew nothing
Of the woes of Christendom, had to protect
Constantinople from the domination of Rome.

LIV

The swan, the water lily on the pond:
Symbols of contemplativity that gives us
Peace, a way to the Kingdom of God.

The eagle and the lightning in high space —
Images of sharp discernment that discriminates
Between the Real and mere dream.

Mysteries that are inscribed in the spirit —
Thou canst see them in God's wise creation.

LV

What the Indians call *wakan*, or
Manitu, is called *kami* by the Japanese:
Firstly, arising from the eastern sea,
The sun: *Amaterasu Ōmi-Kami.*

Kami — the divine in the broadest sense — is power;
Out of this power, essentially, man is born.
Hence the cult of ancestors: man has sworn
Fidelity and adoration to his Origin.

The Divine is fundamentally Ipseity —
The origin of things is the Highest "I";
This coincides with Pure Being —

Hence the primordial law of Shinto: be pure!

LVI

Faith and peace. Faith deep in the heart;
Peace high above, in the realm of thought.
The soul has a root and a crown —
May the Divinity bless the tree of thy spirit.

LVII

Devotion and fervor are the two poles
Of the love of God: devotion is related
To peace; fervor is the ardor of faith;
Wisdom and love are in God's Hands.

LVIII

Two poles: metaphysics and music;
Two abrupt opposites, but also
Related values. For music also has its wisdom,
And wisdom has its hidden songs.

Wisdom can reveal Beauty,
Just as Beauty is the radiation of the True.

LIX

In the picture book of thought, thou shouldst not turn
The pages unnecessarily; it is better to close it.
In this world there is enough thinking —
Behold how God made silence beautiful for thee.

LX

Two opposites: wisdom and woman —
Wisdom is not mere brooding, nor woman mere diversion;
There is no contradiction between the two — the goddess dwells
In the Intellect, just as the Intellect is enthroned in woman.

LXI

In all circumstances, the believer must feel happy
In his heart, so says an adage;
Because God never ceases to be God —
Who would lose courage before the Highest Good?

LXII

Experience, O man, must be. If thou hadst
Nothing of the kind, thou couldst not give much
To others — and there would not be much
For thy soul to show on the Day of Judgment.

LXIV

A samurai, a woman like a butterfly —
Never were there on earth two things more different.
So each of these two unique phenomena had to become
A richly endowed part of the other.

The husband like a freshly drawn sword;
The wife — an ornament of flowers on the hearth.

LXV

Palaces, columns, statues, marble staircases —
Spiritless sumptuosity that will collapse;
Praise be for a simple peasant house
Or a nomadic Bedouin's tent.

The mystery is not that such vain splendor exists —
The mystery is that there are people who like it.

LXVI

One must speak of little things as well as of great ones;
Certainly, one must think first and foremost of the great.
Nevertheless: thou canst not change the nature of the world;
From little things the world is made.

LXVII

The soul is a cup whose content
Is emptiness before the Lord.
God radiates as Truth and Presence —
God's act is never far from pious men.

Like unto a lute is the soul: it is a cup
And a sound, for it owes an answer to the Most High,
And gives it gratefully. God gives the heart peace
And faith, in a world that the heart patiently endures.

LXVIII

Two entirely different things are man as such
And the intellect. The living being is
I and thou; the intellect, God created
That it might perceive the Godhead.

The Intellect may or may not dwell
In a man. The Self alone is.

LXIX

The world of images, which disappears
With the flow of time, wants to live on in our souls,
And continue to dream; it wants, with our substance,
To be born anew, and weave new veils.
Do not give in to this — not too much;
"Rest in peace" — throw illusion into the sea
Of possibility. The Spirit should strive upwards.

LXX

God, the World, the Spirit — three fundamental concepts
That encompass the whole picture of the universe;
Reality, appearance, identity — definitions,
On which thy thinking can rely.
Primordial truths, that deliver from appearance —
May Heaven confer its Grace upon thee.

LXXI

It may happen that our joy in the Most High
Prevents us from having joy in small things;
But on the other hand, it is precisely spiritual joy
That can give the soul some joy in the smallest things.
If thou hast joy in the greatest of gifts,
Thou wilt also have joy in the smallest.

LXXII

It may be that there are now enough songs —
Perhaps I will lay down my pen.
Perhaps: for the decision lies
With Him who is Victor over all.

LXXIII

What we call Spirit is first and foremost the Self
Of the Godhead; then the infallible vision
Of the heart, in angels and in men;
Then reason — purely human understanding.
Just as a word of blessing can penetrate a wall,
So it is with the Self, when it bursts into our thinking.

LXXIV

Fire and snow — a shining duo;
Each one celestial, to each its splendor;
Snow is the peace that has no curiosity;
Fire is the love that supports the Universe.

Thou lovest the sea, whether it roar in the storm
Or subside into its own being;
Thou lovest the dance, not only beauty's stillness;
Both of these — storm and stillness — thou also art.

LXXV

Islam has three formulations which should
Strongly protect man when the world threatens him:
The first one is absolute;
The others are required by our need.

"No God, if not the One" — this is the first.
And then: "What God has willed" —accept it.
And finally say: "Allah is merciful" —
In this way, always carry trust in thy soul.

LXXVI

Circle, triangle, rectangle, line, cross, spiral —
Thou constantly see'st these in things;
Each of these forms is a sign
Whose mysteries reach up to the Godhead.
Symbols of Being, world, and soul;
And also of the Law. See to it, that thy heart choose this.

LXXVII

Perhaps the most difficult thing that confronts thee,
Is to accept the world as it is.
To be sure, one can hardly praise the din of the world;
Nevertheless, much good is woven into it.
Not that thy heart should torment itself with world-illusion —
For it is nothing other than an image of the soul.

Be not concerned about perfection —
Even where it is lacking, it lies deeply hidden.

LXXVIII

The days flow past, and every hour
Brings its rose or thorn.
Song of life — the days go by,
Like flowers that bloom and fade.
Thou art indeed better than the illusion of life —
Against the stream of things thou strugglest in vain;
And many a consolation dries up along the way.
Be still. The rose has the final word.

LXXIX

Life without happenings does not exist —
Even the most holy man must taste events.
And what is more: without the stream of destiny,
The armor of the soul would soon rust.
We have fallen deeply into matter,
Into its consolations and its shame —
Angel and animal, we are in its clutches.
Blessèd the man who has withstood God's trial.

LXXX

Man is like a tree in a river.
He stands there, and the waves lap against him;
He stands because he is what he should be —
Why should the play of things affect him?

It is true that God put him into time;
But not to fade away with things,
Rather to be a witness to the Highest Being —
And, while still in time, to stand in Eternity.

LXXXI

Zeus made the *panta rhei* — the flowing
Of all things — yet He Himself is stillness;
Thus taught Heraclitus. He could tell us
What Zeus made — but not the reason why.

LXXXII

With what wilt thou replace the river of thoughts?
There is nothing more precious than the Scriptures.
And which verse would'st thou choose?
"The Lord is my shepherd; I shall not want."

LXXXIII

Deeds justify spoken words —
Verbal artifice cannot replace deeds.
Truth lies on a knife's edge —
One cannot offend Being with impunity,
Because false witness is an adultery —
Man's speech must correspond to Being.

LXXXIV

That evil exists
        is as clear as daylight;
But why a particular evil should exist,
        one cannot understand.
One accepts it
        because it results from Being —
Because Being's farthest ray
        penetrates even the naught.

LXXXV

God-remembrance is firstly the truth
Of the divine; then it is the great stillness
Beyond the earthly world; then it is the word
Of him who prays and, in it, the Will of God;
Then comes peace — a blissful state —
And then faith glowing within.

Firstly wisdom, which means the True —
And then Selfhood, which attracts us inwards,
And unites us with Truth on the path of Grace.

LXXXVI

One day follows the next, and man
Must think of God at every hour —
He must, in everything he thinks and does,
Give heed to the Will of His Lord.
There is petitioning for Mercy,
And gratitude for God's daily gift thereof;
And, in trial, resignation
And trust that all will turn out for the best.
And love along with fear, and praise and joy —
"He leadeth me to a green pasture."

LXXXVII

When God decides to send a being into the world,
Death already decides to turn the page of life;
And finally, perhaps after a long time, the moment comes —
Then shall the door open unto Mercy.

LXXXVIII

With the rising of the sun comes the day —
Therefore thy day should begin with prayer;
With consciousness that the Most High lives —
Before thou livest, thou shouldst remember this.

LXXXIX

When man turns to God, the evil enemy
Turns to man — he lies in wait
To cause disquiet. Wisdom and prayer
Are a wall of light and love surrounding
Peace of soul. Trials must be;
God will not abandon him who trusts.
In vain does the wicked one seek deceit and war;
The evil one's cunning becomes the victory of the Good.

XC

A Church Father was of the opinion that only man,
And not woman, is God's reflected image;
A pious nonsense — a blasphemy;
Woman is a human being — what else should she be?

Everything in woman manifests the Divine.
In one sense it is man who is the image;
In another sense it is she,
Or it is the couple, that fulfills the Word of God.

XCI

Between God and man is the Prophet
Or *Avatāra*: for men, he is
The Word of God; he is also human speech
And stands as an intercessor before the Divinity.

If ye honor the divine words of the Master,
Then shall God all the more readily hear his intercession.

XCII

The devil wanted to silence the Master —
And so he devised a clumsy ruse:
The Master cannot give judgment on the things
Of this world, because he is too high above it.

"This world": this can be made to include everything;
One will no longer trouble the Master for anything.

XCIII

The Master, they say, is falsely informed —
And so one cannot follow him. One forgets
That he only teaches what he knows with certitude —
And that mastership measures with the measures of God.

XCIV

The enemy of a friend cannot be a friend;
But the enemy of an enemy can be so.
So note well who is thy friend,
And who is the enemy of thy friend — or remain alone.

One's fundamental attitude must be: goodwill towards all;
Then comes discernment between good and evil,
But without passion; for the one who can combine
The world with God, is just.

XCV

When several people share the same destiny,
They do not experience it in the same way;
Different is the inward and different is
The outward; and so one goes round in a circle.

One hardens oneself in one's ego,
And in one's manner of seeing. True vision
Is like dying — and also like living
In Pure Being; a path to the meadows of God.

XCVI

The true sage is a sacrament,
Placed in this lowly world by God;
Fully aware of the essential Truth.
Woe unto him who does not appreciate his spiritual power;

This world has always hated the Light —
But blessèd the man who has grasped Its radiance!

XCVII

The evil one rails against the Most High;
His endeavor ends in defeat.
Meanwhile: helpful is the blessing of the saint,
But God's wrath works through his curse.

There is nothing more terrible than the Master's wrath —
So says a *shāstra.* Whoever feels at ease
In the evil one's claws and deceives himself and the world —
On him will fall the curse of God.

XCVIII

It is not astonishing that the evil one deceives us —
It is astonishing that people obey him,
And that they do so all too readily; instead of seeing clearly
That it is indeed the devil that dares to deceive us.

XCIX

Just as the stars glimmer in the abyss of night,
And Leila's body penetrates the night of her veil —
So should our sense of God and love of God
Shimmer through all cares and sufferings.

The play of a thousand waves may well fascinate thine eye —
The single voice of the sea thou wilt ever hear.

C

Relativity: an oft-used
And misused word — a misunderstanding
Of true values, which are indeed temporal,
But whose primordial contents are eternal.

It is true that earthly things are not divine —
No thing can be entirely absolute.
The play of the world is relative,
Except for one thing: thinking of the One.

CI

"All is vanity," said Solomon —
Strong words. How should we understand them?
The Highest Good always remains true to Itself —
One should not harden oneself in I-and-world.

What we love lies in Pure Being;
What is not worthy of love, is nothing,
And cannot have a lasting effect. In any case,
The world-wheel turns; it is not thy fault.

CII

Canonical prayer — it should come
From within; what thou must say —
What Heaven has prescribed for thee —
Thou must say it out of the joy of thy heart.

For this discourse is like Moses' rod;
So pray with the words God has given,
For He knows man's deepest needs.
Then open thy heart to God, committing to Him
The supplication that burns in thy soul.

CIII

Even if thou art ill and canst scarcely think,
God is thy helper and He thinks for thee;
Patience is everything. God be thy sufficiency —
Even when it seems that the whole world has faded away.

CIV

Who may be the origin of a trial?
The Creator; nature; the evil enemy.
It is God Who permits providence;
The evil one gives nothing, because he always denies.

If God wills suffering — think well on this —
It is because He wishes to bestow on thee thy real Self.

CV

He is the Truth, the whole Truth and nothing but the Truth —
He Who Is, is never sectarianism.
How ye clothe the naked Truth —
This is indifferent to the Most High.

CVI

The meadows are strewn with flowers —
God speaks to us through loving signs;
Just as the songs that a maiden sings
Touch the depths of our soul.

Like flowers are the countless ways
Of love that reveal Divinity;
May our path be like the flowers.

CVII

The thinking of Germanic people is concrete —
The power of the imagination is strongly developed;
Less so with Latins, whose minds
Readily turn to the play of the reason.

Slavs are close to Germans. Semites
Are a priori moralists,
Who delight in the Law day and night —
Their path to God is the effort to obey.

Who are the better men? Gently! Gently!
God willed us, and He knows what He created.

Whatever our origin in the world may be —
Man, as the image of God, is free.

CVIII

The German ambience — this was my earliest world;
Very soon France was added to it.

I also became an Arab and a Red Indian —
True to myself, and according to the way of wise men.

In the present age I felt homeless —
Driven around as on a raft.

The Eternal-Feminine saw me from afar;
The Holy Virgin became my morning star.

CIX

A white man lectured
            a black man saying: "Listen,
You people don't have a Shakespeare;
            so, which of us is greater?
What you Africans lack
            is creative light."
The black man's answer:
            "Are you Shakespeare — or not?"

CX

O man, remain what thou art; do not seek,
Against nature, to become something better.
Women should not be similar to men —
There is enough ugliness on earth.

Ambition and cold reasoning are a curse —
Woman wants to free herself from her lot
And becomes a ghost; but she has no choice:
Only if she is woman can she be a goddess.

Now there are women who are slightly masculine
By nature; those I do not seek to blame;
The world is rich in its play of forms —
Woman should ennoble herself through her mission.

CXI

Youthful beauty is a two-edged sword;
It is decried as vanity or a mere nothing.
It is true that man is not the master of his beauty —
The fact is that beauty is but a loan.

Noblesse oblige. What God has given us,
We must live anew in the Spirit;
The Good from Above must draw us Above —

Imperishable is the blossoming of virtue.

CXII

I know a man who is ninety years old.
His body is as if he had drunk nectar —
It is almost young; with new black hairs in his beard,
With a sharp glance and a strong voice,
He comes forth, immersed in the Eternal Now.

CXIII

"The dogs bark and the caravan passes" —
So said a sage.
If thou standest on firm ground, be confident —
Truth conquers, the dogs bark till they are hoarse.

CXIV

The soul needs light from above,
And then the ability to receive it;
For the God-given light of the Spirit
Wishes to reach an unblemished heart.

From Heaven come God's rays of Light —
So let our breast be the lotus flower.

CXV

A stern angel and a gentle angel may
Stand by thy cradle. The stern one
Is what the Hindus call karma, the obligations
Of destiny — the narrowness of predestination.

The gentle angel is providence, which changes
Everything for the better; and lead is turned to gold.
If thy free soul is directed towards God,
Then the gentle angel will be well-disposed toward thee.

CXVI

Brahma is real, and the world is appearance,
The soul cannot be other than Brahma.
You cannot ask the Primordial Spirit for anything better —
You cannot express the True in a better way.

Then why the doctrinal systems that follow one another,
The Primordial Ideas, and their modalities,
Since the Truth knows no change?
Why is the Unique Word divided?

There are the possibilities of thinking and feeling —
You cannot deny the soul its rights.
Man always wishes to try new ways —
The world-wheel wants the changing play of the times.

CXVII

If thou thinkest of God, thou canst never regret it —
Many another thought will make the soul ill.
Do not forget: everything is in God's Hands —
This world cannot only give good things.

Only the essential counts —
So choose it in thy life's course.
Ephemeral things, as such, are indifferent —
Whenever thou thinkest of God, the Kingdom of Heaven is there.

If thou feelest no happiness in prayer,
It is because thou hast no consciousness
Of God's Nature, which liberates of Itself;
Thou remainest a fool under the weight of the human state.

If the Truth of Itself does not delight thee,
It is because thou wishest to be that which oppresses thy heart.

CXVIII

No man is saved without the Mercy
Of the Lord — so said the Prophet. Someone asked:
Thou too, O Prophet? He replied: Yes, I too —
Only he who, before God, has lamented about himself
Attains to Mercy and salvation —
God is ready to forgive the pious.

Are all human beings bad? No, but learn:
We are born into God-remote existence.
In other words: all beings are included
In the sin of earthly existence.

CXIX

Man's happiness is his peace of soul.
What brings this about? The Truth of the Lord;
And then the Beauty that the soul experiences
When it is at peace under the star
Of the True, and vibrant with love.
Truth and Beauty: keys to peace of heart;
There is nothing better here below.

CXX

The wise man does not need to choose *Advaita* —
It is the primordial fabric of all souls.

In the substance of my heart, Shankar and Krishna
Are deeply and eternally combined.

There is no need to think about merit —
For it pleases the Lord to give Himself freely.

CXXI

The Lord is my sufficiency, it is written,
And His power is of a wondrous kind.
Full of grace is the thought that, already here
In the naught, God has offered me His All.

CXXII

To God belong the most beautiful Names,
Call Him by them — this has been said.
For to God belong the highest qualities;
However ye may call Him — it leads to the One.

And whatever be my way of faith—
The many religions are but one.

CXXIII

Shri Ramakrishna sought to emphasize
The unity, truth, and beauty of the different religions;
He wished to experience every form of faith,
And, through each, to strive towards ecstasy.

CXXIV

Look not, dreaming, into the past
Nor, full of desire, into the question of the future;
What is past, thou canst not change,
And what is to come, God will bring to light.

Be not concerned over joy or sorrow;
Necessity and Freedom — God is both.

CXXV

Bitterness can threaten anyone,
And so can melancholy; both are desired by the evil one,
They are defeat, contrary to salvation,
And incompatible with the nature of the Spirit.

It is as if the psyche were everything.
Take thy refuge in the doctrine of God —
Truth and humility shall deliver thee.

CXXVI

In Japan, *táriki* is the way of
Reliance on the Highest Other.
Jíriki is the way of trust in oneself:
The heart's own-power suffices for the path.

One should not quarrel over this, for what is possible,
Has the right to be, and must be. And each side
Has something of the other: *yin* and *yang*;
Understand the wondrous breadth of the Spirit.

CXXVII

In the West, one calls "philosopher"
The one who trusts in the power of knowledge;
One calls "mystical theologian" the one who
Relies only on love and God's grace.

The philosopher — in Plato's sense — is
The man in whose heart the Godhead thinks.
The mystic — in the sense of Teresa —
Is he whom burning love leads to the Most High.

CXXVIII

The Supreme Name brings the Truth
Of God, and with It, God's Presence.
Man's answer, prayer, is faith,
Coupled with an intention directed towards the Lord.

If thou walkest before God — there are different steps
With which to find the way to the sacred Center.

CXXIX

Fray Gerónimo de la Madre de Dios
Chanted the word "Dios" — it was almost his only prayer.
And it is true that worship in its essence
Consists of the Name of the Most High alone.

Do not forget: in order to tread this path
Thou needest the grace to pray together with God.

CXXX

The realm of gnosis is like the starry heavens —
The realm of love of God is like the song of flowers.
The rigid splendor of the stars affirms the Eternal —
The shining blossoms tell of sweet Graces.

The Way of Knowledge is like the silent night,
For it is mystery and secret depth;
The Way of Love is radiant like the day,
Because it kindles the song-world of our soul.

Gnosis and Love — silence and music;
Yet both bestow the one divine Beatitude.

CXXXI

Thou art Benares, said Shri Shankara —
Thou, cessation of all mental agitation,
Ultimate Peace, and Meaning of all things —
Vairāgya, without burden and without limit —

O heavenly Benares, that I am!

CXXXII

Vairāgya — equanimity. Because what is, must be,
Just as it flows out of All-possibility.
Thou must persevere in God's Eternal Present —
Let the fountain of the world's turmoil gush;
Ultimate Being, in its depth, is silent.

CXXXIII

"In the early morning" — sang Shankara —
"I thought of *Sat*, *Chit*, and *Ananda*;
Of Being, Consciousness, and Bliss — the Three
That transcend the duality of simple thought."

"I am not this body, not this soul —
I am the *Atman* in the cavern of my heart."
That which the Veda calls *Neti-Neti* —
And which the Vedantist knows as "not-this."

"Without birth, without change — eternally
One's Self, Light of the Light — that I am."

Songs without Names

Sixth Collection

She, who silences the river of thoughts,
Divinely soothing mind and soul —
She is Benares, the holy city;
It is she whom I love — and who I am.

Songs without Names

Sixth Collection

I

Fanā and *Baqā* — Extinction and Permanence —
Thus do the Sufis describe our spiritual state
With regard to God; firstly *vacare Deo* —
And then the jewel attained by gnosis.

II

If thou standest before God, then do not rebel,
Even if thy cause be completely just.
In the presence of God,
Let earthly things take their course.

The evil one wishes to unhinge us —
He is not interested in our rights.

III

In my childhood I prayed:
I am small, my heart is pure —
And I wanted always to be
In the garden of the little angels.

Then came hard life,
Things became difficult;
The happiness so near to God —
I no longer found.

But later, Paradise
Opened again —
God finally willed
That my heart be in Heaven.

IV

Somehow nature works better
Than what the hand of man can achieve;
See how the lily in the field
Sings of God, His splendor and His beauty!

The Creator put something of His nature
Into the play of creation:
He gave to flowers something that the world
Of proud human art could never produce.

Sacred art indeed shows evidence of inspiration —
But in nature lies a divine favor
That deeply moves the human soul.

V

In Pure Being there was a possibility,
That said: Give me existence in time.
Existence was granted, and there was my ego;
I said: Thou art my God, now guide me.
God said to me: thou art my image,
And thou art free; say yes to the Way —
The Way to Me; this is the meaning of existence.
I saw that I am the mirror of the Godhead.

Beyond-Being, Being, Existence, I — toward the Most High;
Toward the inmost heart, beyond I and thou.

VI

If one wishes to walk happily on the straight path,
One should perceive the beauty of the True and the Good —
Never forget Plato's words, that the True
Radiates the beautiful, the luminous, the wonderful.

VII

Categories: space and time; form and number;
Cause and effect; substance and energy;
And also quality and quantity. Unnecessary are
The many other things that our mind can conjure up.

A true category is a Sacrament —
Thou canst see in it the pillars of Wisdom;
And, on the basis of the transparency of existence,
Thou canst build a bridge to God's Truth —
And to thy Self — to thine Eternity.

VIII

Life is not like a picture book
That one can leaf through, back and forth.
The past is not in thy hands;
Happiness lies in that which is and will be.

The future is That which no thought can measure.
The meaning of these words — that God is infinite.

IX

Three kinds of attraction: upward, horizontal, downward —
In India these are called *sattva*, *rajas*, and *tamas*;
The horizontal contains the other two within it,
And thus the way divides into two.

Thou seest it in art: horizontal in itself,
It attracts toward both the good and the bad;
In itself art is ordained to deliver the human soul
From the misery of this world.

X

Space and time: ether and energy;
These are not empty, and cannot be so.
Ether contains and energy renews;
Thus the world expands, yet it is but appearance.

Thou art a part of it — and God knows how.

XI

Man is half animal, half angel; something of earth,
And something of the divine. He is pushed to and fro,
But he is one in the Lord, in the silence of prayer.
The soul hears God, and Grace comes from above.

So lead us on the straight path,
Ambiguous as we are. Ambiguity must be,
But also liberation. For God willed us —
As earthly beings that He could liberate.

Useless wavering has affected thy heart;
Flee to God — the door is always open.

XII

If thou speakest with God, and if thine intention is pure —
When thou dreamest not, and thinkest not of this and that —
Then it is God who pronounces His Name,
And makes thee direct thine inmost core toward Him.

XIII

Our life is filled with events,
Which seem great, and which one never forgets —
But which are nothing when we have found the Lord,
When the Lord found us, He who is All and One.

XIV

Man can perceive the whole world,
The farthest stars, even the galaxies —
But these measureless immensities
Do not see us; they are but blind numbers.

Man cannot only see the universe,
He is a glance from God, that transpierces it —
His Intellect can even understand the meaning of existence.

XV

Cause and effect. Take note! The effect is
Contained in the cause like a seed;
In the cause there is a power
That enables the effect to unfold.

In the effect is the substance of the cause,
Good or otherwise.
"By their fruits ye shall know them."
Causality is a mystery that never errs.

Thou seest two kinds of causality in the world:
Firstly, God — and then the possibility
Of darkness or evil, which the Lord allows;
For both act in the ray of the finite,
A ray which, on the one hand, lets the Good shine,
But, on the other, moves away from the Highest Good.

XVI

Form and substance. The substance can be precious through its form,
And the form can be precious through its substance.
Form and number: number adds nothing
To noble form; unless number
Be the meaning of the form — in which case number represents
The value of the thing. Substance and number: Substance
Can be noble, in which case number has worth.

All this is the science of values. And in the
Spiritual life, there are values of this kind —
The One, the Good, the Many. Truth is never new;
Whoever loves God is faithful to all values.

XVII

I have lived through a whole century
And feel as if I am a piece of history —
I have little faith in the majority of men,
But I do not like to sit in judgement.

Because there always are good people in the world.
Whoever loves the Most High respects his neighbor!

XVIII

Firstly, discrimination between *Ātmā* and *Māyā* —
Then concentration on the divine nature of *Ātmā*.
Humility and Faith — then the love-dance of Laila;
Through these the ailing heart can, and must, recover.

XIX

Humility is self-knowledge — objectivity
Regarding oneself. He who knows himself,
Say the Arabs, also knows his Lord —
Such a one separates himself from the illusion of pride.

Humility and Faith go hand in hand —
Faith is to live from the bread of Truth;
It is related to love and happiness,
And frees us from the burden of our weakness.

Know thyself — this is written on Delphi's door;
And have faith, so that thy heart may not be lost.

XX

An event, and not only words,
Is often the speech of the Lord. In order to raise us up,
The Most High tries us with the drink of experience —
One must experience what one has to understand.

XXI

Whether one be eight or eighty —
Joy remains joy and sorrow remains sorrow;
The experience of life changes nothing in this —
Our existence is a contest between these two.

Nevertheless — something can change:
In old age one is no longer entirely on earth.

XXII

Someone saw the Name of God a thousand times
At the same moment — how is this possible, given that God is one?
It is like when early sunlight falls
On the rippling surface of a lake.

There is no multiplicity in God — there is Infinity,
Which, in *Māyā*, is refracted a thousandfold;
The soul has consecrated its all to the Lord.

XXIII

Human language is a kind of miracle —
The fact that one can express ideas with sounds;
From the trivial to the sublime;
From the severe and hard to the sweet and mild.

In words there can be curse, but also blessing;
There is human conversation with its to and fro;
And there is the speech of God, which creates faith.

XXIV

God is Truth, hence consequentiality:
He created His image — so He gave it
Reason and liberty. It is often said that
The Most High owes nothing to the finite —
That it is not right for the earth to complain;
This is true and not true — it goes too far.

Understand: one must not always do what one wants;
And one does not always want to do what one must.
It is not so with God. So be silent.

What is right in itself, the Most High must will —
In other words, He wills that He must.

XXV

Asharī teaches that, if God wills,
He can put bad people in Heaven
And good people in hell; that, since God is free,
Nothing can compel Him to do anything;
That good is only good because God wills it thus;
And that bad is only bad because the Lord condemns it.

Not so! — God is Himself the Highest Good;
And the good is what reposes in His Nature.

XXVI

Divine wisdom, poetry, music,
And feminine beauty are profoundly linked.
Their essence is Truth and Love;
They are nourishment for the Spirit and joy for the soul.

Wisdom blossoms in a wondrous way;
Precious is poetry that points to the Truth;
Noble music is a journey to Heaven;
And beauty is a symbol that leads us to God.

XXVII

How is it possible, that, in the midst of life,
Man can feel sad, even though he is happy?
This can happen because, without knowing it,
He misses Paradise in his everyday happiness.

Man is not made for this world;
Be not astonished thereat, and be on guard!

XXVIII

The Sufis distinguish between *jadhb*, attraction,
And *'irfān*, knowledge;
In the first case, the pious man is drawn upwards;
In the second, God allows him to discern things.
The *majdhūb* lives from lofty heavenly signs —
The *'ārif* reaches God through his Intellect.

XXIX

Certitude of God's Truth; and
Resignation to His Holy Will;
These are the graces and also the duties
That fulfill the meaning of our life's path.

XXX

Credo in Deum Unum — this is the highest;
Blessèd is he who honors God's Truth.
Fiat Voluntas Tua — this comes next;
In this, our soul's striving finds nourishment.

Believing and being resigned: the heart's weapons,
Our viaticum on the way to God — what more couldst thou want?

XXXI

O beata Solitudo, O sola Beatitudo —
The words of St. Bernard. One could also say,
If one may dare to paraphrase:
O beata Certitudo, O certa Beatitudo!

XXXII

David, who danced before the Ark of the Covenant,
And played the harp, and sang the psalms;

Krishna, who played his magic flute,
And, as a god, embraced the gopis;

Shankarācharya, who taught Vedanta,
And whose teaching deeply penetrated India's soul;

Three names that mean infinitely much —
That spread light and warmth into the world.

XXXIII

In this life, unjust opinions
On the part of wisdom-companions are hard to suffer.
Thou askest thyself who they are and who thou art —
Faith in so many things is gone.

What can one do? Alongside the fools there are also the wise —
All-Possibility needs no proofs.

XXXIV

The worst man is not the *shudra*,
Who clings to earthly things, without a heavenward glance —
The worst man is the *pariah*, whose soul
Mixes the lowest with a lofty ambition.

XXXV

Remembrance of God has two dimensions:
The Intellect can contemplate the highest Reality,
And the soul can call for Compassion —
To this the Holy Virgin will readily give heed;
Timeless grace will shine into time.

XXXVI

Beyond-Being, Being, and Existence are
An awesome reality: they are a powerful breathing,
With becoming and unbecoming, with Days and Nights —
Luminous and immutable is the one Eternal.

This thine Intellect can grasp — but thy soul stands
Before Him who created thee; and thou art that
Which will indeed be extinguished — and yet will not pass away.

XXXVII

Sensible consolation is valuable for faith;
But the ascetic would rob us of this solace —
For he is blind to the power of Beauty;
In Beauty he sees not grace — only sin.

We do what the essence of things allows;
What counts is what we love and what we are.
Only the wise man can find light in the realm of forms,
And link earthly things with pure Spirit.

XXXVIII

Why did Shankara, the sage, like to compare
Himself with Benares, the city of Shiva?
The older name of Benares is Kāshī, which means:
The radiant one — the place of bliss.
There the Hindu pilgrim sees the Ganges flow;
Its source is at the feet of Mahādeva —
Shankara carries all this in his nature.
He wants, like Shiva's city, to deliver from illusion.

XXXIX

One may sometimes wonder why God
Grants evil a free play
That goes far beyond the bounds of what one might,
With ordinary reason, understand.

But God enlightens us. The spite of the evil one
Is often a building block for the golden bridge,
Across which the soul returns to her home.

XL

The *pariah* — an unhappy mixture
Of discordant souls — can be dangerous;
Or he can be harmless, without perfidious intent,
A poor fool — one need not shun him.

Those in India "without caste" constitute a whole people;
And many, in the terms of the caste system, are pure.
The differences are relative —
But absolute is God's eternal Peace.

XLI

O Nightingale, what sings thy flute,
On the brink of cool night?
The golden evening light sank down —
The night has brought me peace.

I give thanks unto the Most High —
For He forgets me not.
He, who created day and night,
Is the light of my soul.

XLII

Earthly man has the right to experience many beautiful things —
It is true that he should be above them.
Nevertheless, in what is beautiful in the realm of time,
He should also enjoy the Eternal.

XLIII

When an intelligent man
        speaks with a sharp voice,
It does not necessarily mean
        that he is angry;
Logic and justice
        can sharpen the tone of his speech —
The play of feelings
        is immaterial.

Nobility and Truth
        do not require
That one always behave
        mildly;
Truth is hard —
        one and two are three;
This remains true
        even without a smiling face.

There is a just anger
        that admonishes fools —
No anger is as terrible
        as the rebuke of brahmins.

XLIV

The saving Name, invocation and faith:
This mystery was the heavenly grape
That Hōnen's doctrine pressed; and the juice
Was the wondrous power of salvation.

The Name, resounding from a golden height,
Is what brings the grace of salvation;
Invocation, which seemingly is our action,
Means that we repose in Amitābha's grace.

Faith is everything. Our effort
Is not a merit — it too is God-given.
The message is: we must move upwards
Without thinking that it is we who act.

Tariki, power of the Other;
Jiriki, Self-power. They work in a complementary fashion —
This is the rule that makes the Way perfect.

XLV

What makes man happy? Prayer;
In it lies silence above the world —
Prayer manifests what the ultimate cause is,
And overcomes the weaknesses of our soul.

Contentment in God is a happiness
That places our soul at the Center;
And the intuition of our salvation
Contained in ceaseless prayer makes us happy.

So does thy knowledge that God is one;
And that in Him thou art thy true self.
The enemy's envy must not trouble thee —
Thy heart, O man, is thy beatitude.

XLVI

With David, Krishna and Shankara, we are familiar —
As a fourth name, I could mention Hōnen.
Shinran had more success in Japan,
But the veil of his teaching has a hole:
One cannot repose motionless in grace —
The man who wants something, must do something.
If I only see the grace of a Divinity,
All the rest will melt away like snow.

Shinran exaggerated his point —
But Hōnen, on the path of the golden mean,
Remained faithful to the principle of yin-yang.

XLVII

Monks in West and East sings Psalms
In order to permeate their souls with God.
David could contemplate the Most High in his heart,
And yet he had hundreds of wives;
So everyone who reads the Holy Scriptures
Should see that asceticism is not everything.

XLVIII

Monks too know about matrimonial duties;
But their faith does not know the sentiment
Of beauty in chivalric love —
Hence the opinion that piety is cold.

XLIX

My late father, who played the violin in Oslo,
Had a friend, called Frithjof Thorsen —
A captain on the stormy fjords,
Which promised me a stormy destiny;
For I received this name from the North —
And something of the northern urge for freedom
And its snow-covered paradise.

L

The beginning of God-remembrance is silence
Of the soul, awaiting the fullness of the Godhead —
It ends in the melody of consolation.

It ends? Love of God never ends.

LI

Religion gives us happiness in life,
On the basis of the conviction that life is nothing.
One is happy because one has the right to think with hope
That on the Day of Judgement one will rejoice.

LII

Take thy refuge in the Lord;
                    say not: when I understand everything;
Whether thou understandest or not,
                    thy constant refuge is God.
For He knows thine affairs
                    far better than thou knowest them;
He has all Wisdom
                    and He alone is mighty.
Put what oppresses thee
                    into His compassionate Hands;
Commend thy ways unto the Lord;
                    He will surely take thee under His care.

LIII

Refuge in God may lie in thy will;
If thou speakest to God, know that thou art little.
Seek not in the far off what is quite near —
Refuge in God is already in thy being.

LIV

In the noble man thou findest renunciation,
And this on the basis of God-fulfilled duty;
There is also contentment in God;
And then the profound "yes" of faith.
All this on the basis of the truth that thou thinkest —
And to which, God willing, thou wilt also give thy heart.

LV

The six essential themes of meditation,
I brought into the world many years ago;
But on the other hand — and this I must confess —
The themes of meditation are what made me.

LVI

The men of olden times were wonderful —
So think many admirers of antiquity;
But to the unprejudiced it is clear
That in the domain of sentiments and morals
The men of olden times were scarcely the best teachers.
One must indeed see, if one thinks coolly,
That naïvety often restricted their intelligence.

LVII

I knew a man — wrote Muhyiddin —
Who wept every night over the sins of the day;
His tears flowed over the threshold —
A saint, as people around him thought.
He must have loved his tears immensely,
Otherwise he would not have committed his sins.

LVIII

The penguin wanted a flying contest with the eagle,
And asked: "What wilt thou give me if I win?"
The eagle cares not about things that are too small —
I think I heard him laugh from afar.

"Bird of prey, thou heedest not my proposal.
Very well, proud one, I will teach thee how to dive!"
This is not merely one of La Fontaine's fables —
I have seen the like in the world of men.

When one loses, one tries to avoid being shamed —
It is not difficult, when trying to outdo someone,
To score with a cheap boast.

LIX

Semites greet with: Peace be with thee!
And in fact, peace is essential:
It is repose in God; and it vanquishes
The separation between worlds: between "thou" and "I."

LX

In earthly happenings there are oscillations;
Man is free, and possibility has different levels.
The sage knows what is certainly possible,
But he has no vocation for making prophecies.

LXI

God repented that He had made man;
A strange word — but one sees it in the Bible.
Does it mean that God made a mistake?
Quod absit! But the world contained evil.

LXII

All-Possibility — a word that explains the All,
But not the particular.
The primordial problem is not *Ātmā* but *Māyā*,
Without whose play problems would not exist.

LXIII

If thou believest in God, believe also in thyself—
Which means: believe in thy faith in the Lord.
If God hears me, in a certain way He believes in me —
And this belief of God in me is my good star.

LXIV

Serenity — without petty conditions;
Majesty and Beauty are unconditional.
Extinction in the highest Truth;
Only therein is the human soul great.

There may indeed be greatness in human deeds —
But without God's help man cannot succeed.

LXV

There are many things which are indifferent —
One should not be concerned with them;
And if nevertheless one takes them too seriously,
One should be ashamed before one's Creator.

For these things pass away like dead leaves in the wind —
Thou wilt not take them with thee to the Most High.

LXVI

Vacare Deo — then involvement with things:
This constitutes our earthly life.
And then the combination of both possibilities —
This fabric must also exist.
To see in God and to see God in our seeing;
And so build for oneself a better soul.

LXVII

Time, people say, becomes ever shorter
When one nears the end of one's earthly life;
But, now in old age, I have never felt that
The fates weave their veil more quickly.
For God is always the Most High, and the world is always the world —
So is it also with our soul;
The question is not what destiny weaves —
But on what spiritual ground one stands.

LXVIII

To exist, is to be such and such. If you exist,
You must be this one, and no one else: this particular duty
And this particular destiny. But to realize Pure Being —
You cannot do this in terms of existence.

The petty man, who treats the Spirit like an artistic pursuit,
Should know that there is nothing left for him.

LXIX

From my father came a mystical disposition,
That lived on music, romanticism, and beauty;
And from my mother an energetic nature,
That vibrated for the Real and the True.
Directly from God came an element
That knows a Way to Spirit and to God.

Not without trials is the holy Path;
The wheel of destiny is in God's Hands.

LXX

Stillness in God — I could sing thy praise
Inwardly without end. Just as beauty begets love,
So dost thou bring me the bliss of love —
Even if no other joy remained to me.

Stillness in God — thou hast come to me ever anew;
And so my heart never tires to sing of thee.
Just as the graces given me by God
Resound in my soul day after day.

LXXI

How can one feel joy when one knows
What *Apocatástasis* is —
And *Mahā-Pralaya*? Compared with these,
Our earth is neither hot not cold.

Mahā-Pralaya — the end of all worlds!
Rejoice nevertheless — for this too is nothing
Compared with Beatitude in Pure Being —

Rejoice in the Ray of God's Countenance.

LXXII

There are many people who praise the Most High,
But do not know who the evil one is;
Whoever neither knows this, nor wishes to know it,
Is not armed against satan's ruses.

If, trusting in yourself, you turn your back on him,
Then know, he will certainly be watching you —
To see how capable, intelligent, and strong you are.

An overweening self-confidence
Is not what God asks of us.

LXXIII

What we are, we are through God's Will;
So thou must not desire to be another
As regards race, caste, people, descent —
Whoever denies his origins is base.

How society measures is immaterial;
What counts is what thou art before the Most High.

LXXIV

A Sufi wrote: if one wishes to be alone with God,
Invoking Him alone in a dark cell,
One should first learn to despise everything;
As if the world of pious citizens were hell!

The Sufi wished that one be perfect
Before becoming holy in the *khalwah* —
A pleonasm. The beginning is not the end —
One has the right to be a man made of earth.

It is true that Jesus said: Give not
What is holy unto dogs,
But this does not mean that out of every dog
Thou shouldst studiously make a lion.

LXXV

"What is exaggerated is insignificant" —
Thus one harms the sacred that one seeks to honor;
The language of the ancients is oft misleading —
And yet their intention is praiseworthy.

"What is unreasonable is never law" —
A sage in the East said this to me.
And if human zeal falsifies many things,
One should not accuse the sacred rules.

LXXVI

It seems contradictory that a man
Who loves peace — the universe's harmony
Upon the ground of Pure Being — should also
Respect the warrior spirit, the wild melody
Of the tragedy of existence and its cruelty,
Which mocks so many values in the world;
A contradiction, certainly; yet as a problem
Has this world been made, and so also man.

LXXVII

Priest and warrior. The priest is also
A warrior, when he fights against falsehood;
And the warrior is also a priest,
When, in the world, he spreads the blessing of peace.

Peasant, craftsman, merchant; they are not
Nobility, but they are not insignificant;
The honor of work is the adornment of the citizen;
The peasant is king of our native soil.

LXXVIII

Abstract and concrete: the first is clear to us —
Principles can be grasped by the Intellect;
But the concrete causes us difficulties —
One would often like to escape from its plane.
Certainly, one can understand the essence of things —
But it is difficult to pursue their traces.

What we call abstract becomes concrete,
When our spirit stands on God's ground.

LXXIX

People with the following prejudices
Should never speak of gnosis:
The Most High is similar to man;
One can speak positively only about the will;
There is nothing higher than the law,
So one should torment oneself endlessly with scruples;
One should see in man only the moral element;
The ego is the center in every situation;
One can reduce everything to sentiment;
One should only bewail one's sins.

Gnosis is the vision of That which is —
The vision of the heart, wherein God Himself is the measure.

LXXX

One should not confuse true virtue
With morality — purely outward acts
That change with land and custom,
And do not transform the substance of the soul.

Virtue is inward — it resides in the nature
Of things; its values are the same
From people to people, and in every religion;
Humility, magnanimity and devotion are the paths

That lead from the earthly world to Heaven.

LXXXI

Something that did not exist in earlier times,
Is the overestimation of reason:
It was the wish of the Western world
That practical reason become a divinity;
And so the world of artificiality arose
From a fissure in the cosmic garment —
A latter-day play of All-Possibility.

LXXXII

Existence in itself is completely unstained;
And so is Consciousness. Both will finally
Be freed from the illusion that covers them;
They will be freed from what was alien to them —
And will awaken in the Godhead's radiance.

Thou, earthly creature, let worldly things vanish —
What is divine in thee will not pass away.

LXXXIII

When you call upon the Lord, thoughts come to you
That prove you wish for something else —
But wish for nothing; for it suffices that
With the Lord's Name you calm the tendency to desire.

LXXXIV

Early in my life there came the Psalms, the Bhagavad Gita,
The Upanishads, and Shankara's Vedanta;
Sacred books, my first nourishment —
Then came the free revelation of the Spirit.
A holy shaikh spoke to me about the prayer of the heart —
The profound meaning was the same as Vedanta.
Later life taught me many things —
But everything was given me by the One God.

Stern is the spirit that fights for the True;
But holy wrath is accompanied by music.
Be grateful, pay thy debt to the Most High —
With devotion, humility, generosity and patience.

LXXXV

The soul of a Sufi came to God;
"What bringest thou with thee?" The Most High asked.
The soul replied: "There is but One God —
And this is all I bear with me."

One God alone — rich is the *shahādah*'s meaning.
Abraham's entire message is contained therein.

LXXXVI

When looking at something, what counts first is "what" one looks at;
Then there is the question of "who" is looking;
For instance: the contemplation of beautiful women
Calls for a gaze that is noble and profound.

Likewise: drinking strong, old wine
Calls for the spirit — the sense of Pure Being.
Perception means: know the worth in itself;
Then, be worthy of the object — know thyself!

LXXXVII

Breathing is a symbol: just as, in breathing, the air
Moves inward, so art thou — if nothing in thee resists —
Pulled inward by the Most High;
Thy soul is breathed in by Heaven.

Be conscious of this in every situation —
So that thy soul say "yes" to Heaven.

LXXXVIII

In the idea that God is one
Is contained the thought that the world will vanish —
Then there is the duty of resignation to God's will,
And trust in Him; on these our happiness is founded.

LXXXIX

The oneness of the Most High resounds in the forehead —
But the idea "man" is not contained therein.
Man with God — man's God-experience —
This resounds in the breast, independently of thinking.

The third eye bears witness to the eternal Now;
The eye of the heart raises us up to God —
In it we are true to the purpose of man.

XC

To know that, whatever happens,
Refuge is with the Most High — this belongs to faith;
Nothing has the right, either in the outer world
Or in thyself, to rob thee of thy trust in God.

XCI

There is an ocean of *Māyā* surrounding us —
And another roaring within us.
The Presence of the Most High is a center —
And so is our heart, which hearkens to His word.

XCII

Whoever says *Ātmā*, must think of *Māyā*;
Whoever says *Māyā*, must think of fear and love;
Of duty and grace-given joy — so that nothing
Will diminish the soul's longing for the Most High.

XCIII

There is the treacherous certitude
Which the evil one perfidiously puts into the soul;
Trust it not — and recognize the absurdity
On which the ruse of the evil enemy is based.

Absurd, calumniating, and stubborn
Is the certitude that the devil spits.
Regarding this San Juan de la Cruz wrote:
Be ever ready for humility and for God.

XCIV

Certitude of God is unconditional,
And with it, the peace of soul that it engenders.
Then certitude of salvation — this is conditional,
And so is its peace, when idle doubt keeps silent;
The condition is the Way to the Most High,
And then noble sentiment for one's neighbor —

The love for God that tends towards the other.

XCV

To err is human, but to persevere in error
Because of passion is the diabolic attitude of the fool —
An old saying. Stubbornness is vicious —

But so too is cowardly lack of strength.
To always yield is not a virtue —
Understand: the weakness of the fickle is to no avail.

Only what produces good fruits is good.

XCVI

Warmth pertains to light;
Love pertains to knowledge; for if knowledge
Has not love, it lacks humanity —
The thinker must not separate himself from the human.

And conversely: if love excludes truth,
It becomes foolish and passionately blind —
Love too needs light: it is true to itself
Only when light and warmth become One Love.

XCVII

Man lives because he has been born —
And to live, means to journey towards death.
Why does this dream of life fade away?
Because tired man lives himself to death.

Immortality — a wondrous word:
The flow of life becomes an eternal place
That raises us above the illusion of becoming.

XCVIII

It is not true that old people are spiritually helpless —
Even in the most advanced age one can breathe a prayer.
It is true that everything fades away and becomes more distant —
One has experience; but one cannot make use of it.

XCIX

I was born by a river —
The green Rhine.
There, every day, I saw becoming and vanishing,
And I knew that the river strove toward the ocean —
Just as my soul strives toward limitless Being.

C

Among hard substances thou findest
Raw rock and precious stones;
Likewise with metal: here thou findest lead and gold —
Darkness and light, the coarse and the refined.

So it is in the soul: let the Most High work
In thy spirit — for He can change lead into gold.
Open thyself to God — He will reign in thy heart,
And transmute thine earthly heaviness.

CI

Evolution is nonsense, because the greater
Cannot come from the lesser;
The real — what alone is possible —
Is emanation, conceived by God.

Firstly, one must understand primordial substance —
God wished to sow it on the earthly field.
Can science understand this?
Many things are true which people have never seen.

CII

The earthly field is a poor domain.
One after the other — not one out of the other —
The Lord radiated Ideas into the naught of existence —
The possibility of man
Never emerged from the animal.

For the good reason that the Creator — heed this well —
Made us human beings according to His image:
Before the All-One, no other one was there —
Being did not arise from anything else.

CIII

"There are more things in Heaven and on earth
Than are dreamt of in your philosophy" —
Said Shakespeare. But who wants to become a sage?

Too many things seem self-evident to man —
He was born in them, grew up in them,
And thinks his poor day-to-day existence has to be.

Divine possibility is infinite;
And out of it our world was made.

Man kindled his own dream —
The foundation of existence can be grasped by the Intellect alone.

CIV

"Say: God — and leave them to their idle prattle" —
A verse from the Koran. Thou shouldst strive
Toward the Great One — who is the meaning of thine existence
And thy happiness. And life is simple.

CV

For some, the cause of spiritual happiness
Lies in a sacred idea, in primordial thought;
For others, it is in experience and sentiment —
So let us thank God for both light and love.
The paths are diverse, but the goal is one.

CVI

Truth is not always what one wishes.
When one is stubborn in one's opinion,
One must die before Reality,
Just as the soul ripens towards salvation.

Our desire waits — and Truth also waits
For man to respect its holy rights;
As thou treatest the truth,
So shall God — the Good Shepherd — treat thee.

CVII

Character or technical skill:
It is the first that makes the man — not the second.
Inventive genius does not constitute nobility of soul;
The best is not always the white man.

Technocracy ruins the human soul —
I do not give this opinion lightly.
One found many noble people amongst the barbarians,
As they were fifty summers ago.

CVIII

The master of ceremonies of a prince told me:
Many guests once came to a festival:
People of princely lineage
From many countries, gentlemen with their ladies.
Two women amongst them talked together in a low voice —
The master of ceremonies, pale-faced, ran
And whispered into the ear of one of them:
In the presence of the prince, we are as nothing.

If this is so in the world of men —
It is immeasurably more so in the presence of God.

CIX

A Red Indian chief said to a missionary:
We have prepared our souls with our tobacco;
And the smoke of our Pipe carries our prayers to Heaven.

The White man knows not the Red Man's tradition:
That one never quarrels about the Great Spirit.

CX

Hope for salvation — its symbol is the future,
Because ahead of us lies what has still to come;
On the other hand, it is a "yes" to God,
If our heart is full of deep faith.

The future, which draws our soul Heavenwards;
The same hope, but experienced differently:
Inwardness, which sees God in the heart.

CXI

Man does not belong entirely to this earth;
He was expelled from Eden's gate;
He fought hard to be forgiven —
Yet he must live as an earthly animal.

Faith dispels all guilt.
Do not forget that in Heaven's heights
The pure and blessed are also men.

CXII

Necessity and accidence: these are
The two levels on which people walk;
This makes them what they are:
It shapes their willing, feeling, experience, and deeds.

Each of the two levels has degrees:
Necessity and possibility can show themselves
In things both great and small; the small must
Be what it has to be, and be silent before the great.

So put everything in its proper place —
This is the first sentence of the wisdom of life.

CXIII

Man is a mixture of luminosity and heaviness —
"Of earth thou art and unto earth thou wilt return,"
Thus spake God to man. He spoke of life's garment,
And not of the spirit or immortality —
From God's light, no earth can arise.

CXIV

The youth who loves a noble maiden
Wants endlessly to praise her charms;
He never tires to sing of Laila,
And asks not what this gives to others.

Likewise the mystic, who repeats
What gives joy to his soul:
No wonder, that in his love of God,
He repeats life-long the self-same words —

Just as the circle — never weary of its rotation —
Has no beginning and no fading away.

CXV

One should not praise the day before the evening —
So goes a popular saying. And rightly so;
But there is one exception — when the day's activity
Has one intention only: our way towards the Above.

CXVI

Thou shouldst not blame the evening in the morning —
This also is true. Live in the eternal now —
In God's presence. Thou hast the day
Wherein to plow the field of thy salvation.

One also says: all's well that ends well;
For all endings rest in the Divinity.

CXVII

There are two things no one can take from us:
The Now in God — already in this earthly time;
And then the All-Merciful's last word,
From which we are created — but in eternity.

CXVIII

Do not forget that the Now does not belong to thee —
Only God is worthy of this unique Miracle.
And yet He has also given it to thee —
He who leads the soul toward His very Being.

CXIX

In the word dwells something of the thing named,
If it is a primordial word in a noble language;
The Most High's Presence in His Name —
The human word is a framework for this power.

The uncorrupted Word is Revelation,
Not human work; it is given by God for the preservation
Of the Divine Truth. Hold It in honor,
Thus will the sacred sound convert thy heart.

CXX

One was afraid of something without reason —
What came to pass was good. One is ashamed
Before the Creator, who directs everything.
He is the fashioner of destiny, from our first breath to our last hour.

To think of that which may or may not be
Is useless, and contrary to faith.
Thou shouldst not put thy trust in dreams —
Close thine eyes and trust in God.

CXXI

God says "yes" — the yes of His Reality and Presence.
And I say "yes" to God —
The yes of submission and security;

No sooner have I awoken than the Lord is there.

CXXII

Desiring pulls the soul hither and thither —
In God alone can it find repose.
Desiring has indeed a certain natural right
To action — but worldliness
Cannot link us to Paradise.

So desire nothing when God beats in thy heart —
Then desire's energy will become, not what it craves,
But what it contains in its primordial substance.

Blessèd the man who turns to pure Love.

CXXIII

Sunrise: the sun rises in the sky —
This is how our eye sees it, but not science.
For science, the sun does not rise,
Because the light of the heavens is motionless.

But what we see — God wanted us to see
And believe. Because God alone —
In the All-Possibility that belongs to Him —
Is the eternally and divinely Immovable.

What science, for its part, sees and measures
Is true, and so it bears witness,
In its own way, to the absolutely Real.
As does also the rotation of the earthly ball,
Image of the relativity of outward seeing —
Image of the relativity of the created universe.

CXXIV

It is said: the morning hour has gold in its mouth;
And this is true, not only because of our work,
But above all if, with the first ray of sun,
Our thoughts are directed toward Heaven.

CXXV

Lower *Māyā* is materiality:
It is only of earth, and not of the Spirit;
Higher *Māyā* is supra-materiality —
Primordial and universal Substance, which shows the way toward God.

Evolutionist delusion: the root of the error is
That it measures with the measures of matter:
That it seeks the cause on the earthly plane,
And thereby forgets the breadth of the Cause.

CXXVI

Dawn breaks and the sun rises
In a rosy light;
Thus does the Lord, veiled and from afar,
Show His Face;
And thou rememberest in thy heart
The Light of God;
And whatever thy neighbor's destiny, joy or grief —
Forget it not.

CXXVII

Mere appearance and reality
In nature
Are in fact not contradictions —
It only seems so;
So doubt not God's work — blessèd is he
Who forgets not
That everything in the earthly and heavenly worlds
Is a symbol.

CXXVIII

Some think that he who strives for personal salvation is selfish —
That one should also obtain salvation for one's neighbor.
This one cannot and need not do; for one's own salvation
Has a radiation that gives life to others —

On their path to inherit the Highest Good.

CXXIX

If something petty annoys and troubles thee,
Thou wilt hear in thy heart: Hold fast to Me!
Because what for Me does not exist at all —
A speck of dust from the world — should be for thee a naught.

CXXX

Hinduism is a whole world;
Here thou canst find what pleases — or does not please —
Thy spirit. The Absolute, the One,
Is what Vedanta teaches — It knows no idols.

Then came Islam, which knows only Unity,
And which calls only the One its Divinity;
No wonder that in the land of Vedanta,
So many found pleasure in the Koran.

CXXXI

Logic is right thinking. But not only this —
Because, before mental concepts, comes right being;
Truth is not merely what we wish to think of it —
Clear thinking must be the trace of the things themselves.

The prototype for our consciousness is the nature of things;
One cannot separate mental forms from primordial Being.

CXXXII

Hinduism — a spiritual world
That contains everything, and shimmers in all colors;
It offers us Vedanta, the doctrine of the great Shankara:
And also gods without number,
In whose cult our heart has no interest.

Islam wants first and foremost to be Unity,
And life-wisdom. It also knows the wine
Of the heart, that turns the soul inwards.
Islam is revelation's last sanctuary.

In whichever language one honors truth:
God is Reality — the world is appearance.

CXXXIII

It is often said that the joy of love
Is but a fleeting dream: this is true and not true.
Whatever is in time rushes past like time itself;
But whatever therein is eternal remains miraculous —
Deeply embedded in the melody of Being,
The melody that was before the earthly dream.

CXXXIV

The tree grew up from root to crown;
It was made for someone to dwell in:
And indeed, Heaven's nightingale
Crowns its crown with its sweet sounds.

The human soul is like a tree,
That unfolds through the Will of the Most High.
May something from Heaven
Crown the tree of the soul, and fulfill the meaning of its existence.

CXXXV

Beauty is timeless, eternal, said Rumi wisely;
For beauty belongs to the Lord, it is not of this earth.
And Beauty herself testifies
To her divine nature — but she says it gently.

CXXXVI

God does not need us — we men need Him,
So that the power of evil overcome us not.
But God cannot be without creation,
For radiation lies in the nature of God.

So one can say: God could not not create,
For where there is sun, there must be radiation —
But only within the world-dream, home of duality,

For God alone is Pure Reality.

CXXXVII

It is strange that we must plod through life —
Could we not, like flowers, just look upwards?
All-Possibility wanted us as human beings —
So we must greet God in our own way,

And trust in the Lord's blessing.

CXXXVIII

Pandora's box is the potentiality
Of evil. Whose was the wicked deed?
The box was opened, in order to show
What deluded man has ruined —
Only vain hope remained hidden therein.

God gave us true hope — His morning.

CXXXIX

"Sculptor God, strike me, I am the stone"—
Thus spoke Michelangelo as poet.
He knew well that in life trials must be,
And that the Most High is the Judge.
"If only Dante's lofty soul had been bestowed on me"—
Trials lead to ultimate peace.

CXL

God's morning: when the sun rises
You know that the day will unfold.
So it is with the hope of salvation,
When the earth bows down before the light —

God wants to shape anew the soul of man.

CXLI

There is the drunkenness of the noble and the beautiful —
Nature and poetry; wine, woman and song.
Then there is the drunkenness of the pure void —
Blessèd art thou if thou hast found the way thereto:
If, beyond thine earthly experience,
Deep in thy heart, God's sound has reached thee;
If, by God's grace, thy spirit's strength
Has wrested from thine I its sacred Content.

CXLII

Seeming paradises — men who are but accidents
Experienced them and dreamt of them. Play of possibility
On the edge of nothingness; half grace, half childishness —
Dream on, O men; thus does time pass
With its years, months, days, hours.

There are many for whom the Lord has shattered illusion
In the light of Ultimate Reality.
The path to the meaning of life's dream is long —
And yet perhaps not; nothing better has ever been found.

CXLIII

It is remarkable how many animals are sensitive
To spiritual ambience, and love the sacred;
For instance, Rumi's cat, which, it is said,
Went to Heaven; God wished to manifest a grace.

This is so, because animals of all kinds
Carry within them something of the nobility,
Childlikeness, and even piety, of man;
And so the Lord, who knows all hearts,
Is ready to perform an unusual act of grace.

So shouldst thou too respect modest creatures,
Which — without knowing it — tend towards the Most High.

CXLIV

Sattva, rajas, tamas: light, heat, heaviness;
Gold, copper, lead; and, in man,
The upward tendency, then passion,
Then baseness, wherein no pity is.
Heat has a double face:
It comes from the evil one, or it is light.

All this thou must carefully discern,
Both in creatures and things —
And react to every aspect as befits its nature.

The three *gunas*, which manifest the play of Being —
In *Māyā's* household, they are always combined.

CXLV

Men have difficulty in understanding
That God's door is always open;
They live carelessly — which means they stand
On the shaky framework of their existence,
And scarcely know where to turn.

I want to say it time and time again:
It is not difficult to venture into the presence of the Lord.

CXLVI

Devotion — hast thou understood this word aright?
Devoted is the lotus on the pond,
And the swan that swims thereon in circles —
Many primordial symbols bear witness to the kingdom of Heaven;
See also the weeping willow, which bends towards
The surface of the water — silent in devotion.

Devotion means: to think upon — but with the inmost self;
For it is with the Heart, which sees the Most High,
That thou shouldst remember Pure Being.

CXLVII

One could talk endlessly of beauty,
For in its holy nature it is infinite;
As is also knowledge. And blessèd is the heart
That does not forget Plato's ray of Beauty in the True.

CXLVIII

What is the I — who has woven this dream
Which belongs to me and to no one else?
And which nevertheless longs for the other,
In whom, through love, it may forget its misery.

Am I the veil of memories —
The being who senselessly seeks distraction —
Who is helplessly dragged through time,
And wishes to miss and to regret nothing?

Am I the one who wishes to preserve himself,
And does not want to understand that everything is appearance?

I am myself only in God's Word —
Which causes me to awaken in Pure Being.

CXLIX

All too often psychology replaces logic —
Even Truth itself —
And has thereby, in our decadent age,
Robbed many people of all support.

Had one remained with Aristotle,
One would not have swallowed every false idea —
Psychomania twists everything according to its will.

CL

One should not fear what the damned one whispers —
Which, though it is but miserable absurdity,
Can yet darken the human soul —
But the perfidy of the evil one passes away.
No matter how foully he behaves —
Afflicting the pious never brings him profit.

God wishes to keep the good man in humility;
And therefore — whether one understands it or not —
He allows a certain play to hellish powers.

CLI

It is taught that sociology is everything —
Whereas one barely knows what one is talking about.
Society has meaning only when it corresponds
To the image of the chivalrous friend of God.

CLII

"There is no duty higher than Truth" —
This is the maxim of the Maharaja of Benares.
It is a principle that contains the whole world —
For without Truth, the human state is worthless.

CLIII

The vehicle — in the world — of the Absolute
Is relative like the world itself;
But his Divine Word, which is absolute,
Causes the Absolute to descend upon him:
"Guru is Brahma" — because the bearer of Divinity,
Through Brahma, illumines all darkness.

CLIV

The Master, a voice from the Absolute,
Dwells like others, like the whole world,
In relativity; but his vocation
Causes the Absolute to enlighten him,
To give him graces, and to clothe him in wisdom.

Thus could Shankara Benares be.
"Guru is Brahma" — guru is the miracle
Which in the world separates light from darkness.

CLV

Wisdom and faith are considered opposites —
But not always. Knowledge of the sacred
Requires faith; for man's soul
Must participate deeply in the light of the Spirit.

To the discernment between *Ātmā* and *Māyā*
Pertains realizatory faith — *shraddha*;
The soul must sanctify knowledge.

CLVI

A good man did something clumsy —
Some said that his intention was wicked.
And this opinion, which chooses the bad,
Is a thousand times worse than the deed
That one slanderously calls in question.

CLVII

The fool holds the science of *Ātmā* in his hand —
But to the wise man, *Ātmā* is unknown.
The fool may call the Most High whatever he wants —
But only the Most High can know Himself.

Do not take this too literally; it is clear
That every wise man knows *Ātmā*.
In this case, why the contradiction? To show
That the truest word about the True is silence.

Why then say that *Ātmā* is infinite?
That one must say it, is self-evident.

CLVIII

Everything which, in the customs of many peoples,
Constitutes a cruel absolute means
That both in one's actions and in one's soul,
One must carry the greatness of noble ancestors.
It is believed that man is what he strives towards,
And that the community will degenerate quickly
If it does not walk in the tracks of the ancients —
If it does not experience the Absolute.

CLIX

Thinking lives from what is real;
No man is inclined to think of pure nothingness.
Given that thy guiding star is the Real,
Why wilt thou not commit thy thinking
To That which signifies the Highest Reality?
For God's Light is an easy burden.

CLX

Bhagavad Gita, the Song of the Exalted One —
Even as a child I loved it, for it meant India,
And because it resounded in my own language;
It is no wonder that I was reading in it
When the greatest spiritual grace of my life entered into me.

CLXI

In this world, there is always something to ponder —
The question is whether it is worthwhile
For the human spirit, which is made for God,
To be consumed with foolish adiáphora.

Thou shouldst know: when thy soul reposes in the Most High,
He will be with thee, and will tell thee
What is worth thinking about and what is not;
What is useful in thy life's path, what is vain, and what is good.

CLXII

One should distinguish between a defect
And a weakness; I call the latter harmless,
And the former harmful, an offense to God.
Weaknesses there may also be in Paradise —

For man has the right to enter Heaven;
God allows His children to be human.

CLXIII

The sense of the great is an ideal —
But be careful lest everything become false and artificial.
In princely courts there are exaggerations —
The mania for greatness can only make men little.

Pride and stubbornness make great things small —
One can be noble without suicide.

CLXIV

The world is full of injustices
That bring sorrow to body and soul.
If everything rested in the Will of the Most High,
St. Michael would not have much to do.

It is said that everything is in God's will —
But the word "will" has different meanings.
If everything that happens were agreeable to the Lord,
He would never have to be wrathful with man.

CLXV

Holiness — this is the first greatness;
But greatness is not always holiness.
A sense of the sacred is the first step —
The goal is near, and yet the way is long.

CLXVI

Trust in thy good star —
The Way may be short, even if thou see not the goal,
And imagine it to be infinitely far.

It may happen that a miracle will triumph:
If this lies in thy very substance,
And is thy destiny — if it please the Lord.

CLXVII

The world is a play of enigmas. One must understand
People in their ambiguity —
In thy God thou shouldst always trust,
And know that He is unambiguous,
And will accompany thee on all thy paths
Amidst the human drama. Under His protection
Thou canst rest peacefully and without sorrow.

CLXVIII

That earthly people are what they are,
Not more, not less, every child knows.
The evil one, who makes people worse,
Has brought many a one into the net of absurdity.
Thou must never be subjective;
Reason and trust in God will liberate thee —

The grace that keeps watch in thy heart.

CLXIX

The Lord certainly does not demand
That we not call a scoundrel by his name.
But He does require us to see
The attenuating circumstances and limits
In the sin of a good man.
For, as we measure here on earth,
It will be measured unto us in the hereafter.

CLXX

Love, indifference, scorn, hatred —
The last is utterly against God's Will;
The first thou findest in the Lord Himself:
In love thou wilt fulfill His commandment.

Indifferent to the soul is all that has no meaning;
Scorn is rejection, it is not hatred.
All this lies on the plane of feeling —
Thou must apply the criteria of the Spirit.

CLXXI

It is very difficult to bear absurdity;
But one must become accustomed to the senseless —
The human soul cannot groan a whole life long
Because of the ugliness of nonsense,

And long in vain for paradises.
The remedy is never to forget
That God is the rock of pure Truth —

The Quintessence of the good and the beautiful.

CLXXII

Amongst wise men there are some
Who were scorned in their youth;
What does this absurdity mean?
It is the play of destiny's alchemy,
Which espouses this or that form;
Out of a misunderstood duckling arose
A proud swan, as Andersen relates.

God wishes to unfold many possibilities —
In the form of our destiny a deep meaning is contained.

CLXXIII

Life — a mixture of good and bad;
Evil cannot be ignored.
From whatever direction the winds may blow —
Man cannot dispute with his destiny.

To see the good means gratitude;
When the bad depresses thee too much,
Think first of God, then of the grace
That makes thee happy amidst the dream of life.

CLXXIV

Say nothing false, hide nothing true —
Said Cicero. Which strictly speaking means:
The truth, the whole truth, and nothing but the truth —
It also means whatever points to the essence of things.

It is not facts as such that are important —
More important is what they mean.

CLXXV

Man is not only thinking, he is also willing,
And what he thinks, must have willing as a consequence;
Otherwise thinking is mere play,

And an attempt to flee from the Real.
Where there is Truth, there is also Reality —
One should see the True as Real.

To know is also to love — to love whatever
Bears witness to Divinity. Whoever loves God,
Will not be abandoned by the All-Merciful.

CLXXVI

Human language? Words are too narrow;
A word often contains a whole sermon,
But it remains unnoticed. Therefore sages make
Heavenly wine out of pale earthly water —
When they elaborate with a commentary,
What wills to be expressed in one word alone.

CLXXVII

The Name "All-Merciful" must be understood aright —
It does not mean that there is no burning hell,
It means that for the one who has found Him
God forgives everything that people call "sin."

Blessèd the man who has overcome a difficulty —
A trial, which often knows no mercy,
Is the holy price of our highest path.

CLXXVIII

Flowers on the ground and stars in the sky —
Flowers shine by day and stars by night;
Flowers fade away, whereas stars are everlasting —
From a human point of view — and shine from afar.

Spirit, soul — songs in time;
Above there is silence — the song of eternity.

CLXXIX

I think again and again of how
Tiruválluvar gazed at the temple
From afar; as a *pariah*, he did not have the right to enter —
He heard the distant sounds of worship.

The slightest sign that reminds us of God
Is immensely more than our soul can imagine.

CLXXX

What this earthly life is,
            one only knows at the end.
If one lives this life until death,
            it is because one must.
Man has no right to be ungrateful —
            so many things were beautiful.
But one who has been totally happy —
            thou hast never seen.

CLXXXI

To the extent that thou believest that earthly things,
Good and bad, are in God's hands,
To that extent, sorrow will be far from thee;
God can change life's course for the best.

If thou thinkest of God, think of nothing else;
Only God's Being and Truth are important —
God will send thee solace out of His very Nature.

CLXXXII

At every moment, direct the steps of thy soul
Towards thinking of the Lord.
If thy soul tires of this,
Then what thou doest is not God-remembrance.

Have I not often said that during prayer
Of the heart, God's door is open?
So let us steep our heart in His Word.

Notes

Notes to *Songs without Names V*

1. *Gottfried* = Peace of God
   Gottlob   = Praise of God
   Gotthold   = Favored by God
   Gottlieb   = Love of God
   Fürchtegott = Fear of God

Index of Foreign Quotations

Adventum regnum tuum (Latin): "Thy Kingdom come" (Lord's Prayer) (p.152).

Allāhu karīm (Arabic): "God is bountiful" (p.77).

Brahma satyam (Sanskrit): "God is real" (p.179).

Cogito ergo sum (Latin): "I think, therefore I exist" (p.5).

Credo in Deum Unum (Latin): "I believe in one God" (The Nicene Creed) (p.262).

Di fresca verdura; / genti v'eran con occhi tardi e gravi, / di grande authorità ne' lor sembianti: / parlavan rado, e con voci soavi. (Italian): "...A meadow of fresh verdure; / people were there with solemn eyes and slow, / of great authority in their countenance; / they spoke seldom, and with gentle voices." From Dante's *Divina Commedia, Inferno IV.* 112-114 (p.143).

Eppur si muove (Italian): "But it does move"; attributed to Galileo, leaving his interview with the Pope in which he had been forced to recant the theory that the earth moves around the sun (p.196).

Errare est humanum (Latin): "To err is human" (p.215).

Felix culpa (Latin): "Happy fault" (p.10).

Festina lente (Latin): "Hurry slowly" (p.43).

Fiat voluntas tua (Latin): Thy Will be done (Lord's Prayer) (p.262).

Lā ilāha illa 'Llāh (Arabic): "There is no divinity but God" (p.80).

Ma già volgeva il mio disio e il velle / l'Amor che muove il sole e l'altre stelle. (Italian): "...But already my desire and my will were revolved / ...by the Love that moves the sun and the other stars." From Dante's *Divina Commedia, Paradiso XXXIII.* 143-145 (p.196).

Mā shā'a 'Llāh (Arabic): "What God has willed" (p.77).

Mea culpa (Latin): "Through my fault" (p.10).

Muhammadun Rasūlu 'Llāh (Arabic): "Muhammad is the messanger of God" (p.80).

O beata Certitudo, O certa Beatitudo (Latin): "O blessèd certitude, O certain Beatitude" (p.262).

O beata Solitudo, O sola Beatitudo (Latin): "O blessèd solitude, O sole Beatitude"; St. Bernard (p.262).

Om namo sarva Tathāgata Om (Sanskrit): "Hail to those who are 'thus gone'" (p.49).

Panta rhei (Greek): "All things flow"; Heraclitus (p.231).

Prudenter agas, finem respice (Latin): "Act prudently and think of the result" (p.43).

Quod absit (Latin): Literally: "Which would be absurd" (i.e., "Perish the thought") (p.273).

Se non è vero, e ben trovato (Italian): "If it is not true, it is nevertheless well invented" (p.176).

Theòs estin (Greek): "God is" (p.6).

Vacare Deo (Latin): "To be empty in God" (pp.146, 253, 274).

Vox populi, vox dei (Latin): "The voice of the people is the voice of God" (p.174).

Index of First Lines

A book about the Sufis of Andalusia: 125
A child who has been burned… 187
A Church Father was of the opinion… 233
A good man did something clumsy — 305
A great commentary on the Brahma-Sutra — 183
A guiding thought comes to my mind: 164
A man recited ceaselessly his prayer — 63
A noble man is he who thinks objectively, 59
A prejudice is idle self-deceit — 85
A prince gives a castle to a saint; 125
A proverb says: it is too beautiful to be true; 181
A Red Indian chief said to a missionary: 289
A saint weeps over his sins — 126
A samurai, a woman like a butterfly — 226
A stern angel and a gentle angel may 242
A Sufi wrote: if one wishes to be alone… 277
A symbol is the water lily 29
"A universal demolisher": people called… 134
A villain hates thee — and yet 69
A white man lectured 240
A winter fairy tale. Snow covers the land — 80
A wise man said: ask yourselves — who am I? 8
A woman gives birth to a child: if it is a son — 132
Abstract and concrete: the first is clear to us — 278
According to Plato, knowledge is recollection. 176
Adam and Eve; and then the Fall. 220
After nearly two thousand years 148
Al-*Hallāj* said that he was God — who knows 67
All in all: most poets 13
"All is vanity," said Solomon — 237
"All is vanity," said Solomon. 170
All the images of the world rush into thee 120
All too often psychology replaces logic — 303
All-Possibility — a word that explains the All, 273
All-Possibility: from it stem the many things 7
Al-Qutb — the Pole, it is called in Sufism; 70
Although I am indebted to Shankara, 20
Among hard substances thou findest 285
Amongst wise men there are some 310
An angel spoke: thou shouldst not be sad; 121
An enigma of destiny is man's activity: 50
An event, and not only words, 259
An over-clever man once wrote: 136
And many believe that thinking is enough — 176
And when ye pray, use not many words, 192
Angustia — fear of life: this is a madness 58
Are there flames that blaze eternally? 32
As a child, I once imagined I was in 66
As is the language, so is the religious form: 90
As sparks flash forth in the cold night 46
Ashari teaches that, if God wills, 261
Ask not the question: what is going to happen? 67
At every moment thou canst find refuge… 155
At every moment, direct the steps of thy soul 313
At the end of all time and all worlds, 83
At the end of time, the Prophet said, 201

Bad character is responsible for itself, 186
Be careful before ye reject faith; 57
Be happy because God is Truth and Peace; 173
Be not surprised that Krishna, Abraham, 24
Be not surprised that, when the devil threatens 31
Beauty is timeless, eternal, said Rumi wisely; 297
Being has power, it can negate Itself — 112
Between God and man is the Prophet 234
Between the earthly man and the Lord, 200
Beyond-Being, Being, and Existence are 264
Beyond-Being, Being, Existence: 197
Bhagavad Gita, the Song of the Exalted One — 306
Birds that cry out the Supreme Name, 135
Birth and death — two shores, and a sea 120
Birth, and then death — this is one thing. 5
Bitterness can threaten anyone, 245
Blind obedience and nobility of soul 189
Blue means depth, contemplativity; 18
Brahma is real, and the world is appearance, 242
Brahmin, kshatriya — the difference 172
Breathing is a symbol: just as, in breathing… 281
Build the temple, not the Tower of Babel; 35
"Burn what thou hast adored," 37
Canonical prayer — it should come 237
Categories: space and time; form and number; 255
Cause and effect. Take note! The effect is 257
Certainly nomadic people must hunt — 161
Certainly the warrior's profession must exist, 161
Certitude is Being, when it is reflected 7
Certitude of God and then certitude… 221
Certitude of God calls for nobility of soul 191
Certitude of God is also certitude of salvation, 14
Certitude of God is unconditional, 283
Certitude of God's Truth; and 262
Character or technical skill: 288
Christians and Saracens murder each other — 216
Circle, triangle, rectangle, line, cross, spiral — 229
Cogito ergo sum — the fact that humans think 5
Confucius taught that everything is reason 214
Consecrated water and consecrated wine — 123
Co-operation, and yet opposition, 179
Country and history — deceiving hells; 165
Credo in Deum Unum — this is the highest; 262
Dante's language makes Latin milder; 124
David danced before the Ark of the Covenant; 194
David was not only king and prophet, 151
David, who danced before the Ark… 263
Dawn breaks and the sun rises 294
Death: no one can reach pure Being 119
Deeds justify spoken words — 231
Delight in the many, longing for the One: 95
Depth of spirit — this is accompanied 78
Desiring pulls the soul hither and thither — 293
Despise not what artists of this world 76
Devotion — hast thou understood this word… 302
Devotion and fervor are the two doors 169

Devotion and fervor are the two poles   224
Dialectic and music — since my earliest days   104
Didst thou see the morning sun on the snow,   80
Dignity and self-domination have disappeared   158
Divine wisdom, poetry, music,   261
Do not believe that Shri Shankara was God —   179
Do not do several things at once   116
Do not forget that the Now does not belong...   291
"Double truth," was the Medieval term: 28
Dreaming from my father, energy from...   98
Each poem has its own argument—   39
Each poem has its own argument—   55
Early in my life there came the Psalms...   280
Earthly man has the right to experience...   266
Either thou dwellest in a cave   211
Eppur si muove — is it true that the Earth   196
Errare est humanum. Thou shouldst not   215
Europe's folk art is one of the best things   217
Even if thou art ill and canst scarcely think,   238
Even the sages who did not condemn...   24
Every day, the Sufi has three thoughts: 164
Every happiness is a distant ray   117
Everything which, in the customs...   305
Everywhere there is the risk of misusing...   44
Evolution is nonsense, because the greater   286
Exaggeration, even pious lies —   148
Excess lies in human nature;   103
Exegesis of the Holy Scriptures: take care   126
Existence in itself is completely unstained;   280
Existence is like walking on a mountain: 138
Existence: constructed of a thousand things —   144
"Existentialism" is a thinking   69
Experience, O man, must be. If thou hadst   226
Faith and peace. Faith deep in the heart;   224
Faith is the spiritual strength   71
Faithfulness — a quality of gold —   117
False science has no limits,   137
Fanā and *Baqā* — Extinction and Permanence   253
Faqir, "one who is poor,"...   74
Fata Morgana — is it not an illusion?   81
"Father, forgive the sinners, for they know not"   43
Fire and snow — a shining duo;   229
First *certitudo*, then *serenitas* —   184
First the Name of God: presence   138
First Truth, then patience. The one   14
First, discernment, and then concentration.   222
First, Shri Shankara — he is the greatest;   163
Firstly, discrimination between *Ātmā*...   258
Flowers on the ground and stars in the sky —   312
Fools think that in Heaven,   177
For Dante, all wise heathens   143
For some, the cause of spiritual happiness   287
Form and substance. The substance...   258
Formerly it was believed that the sun and   133
Fray Gerónimo de la Madre de Dios   247
Freedom — but within the framework...   173
From my father came a mystical disposition,   275
From the horse comes that kind of soul   20
Genius is nothing, if not combined with...   137

"Give us," said Jesus, "our daily bread":   177
God does not need us — we men need Him,   298
God doeth what He wills, and wills what...   73
God gave the earthly pilgrim a bowl   94
God grant that I may speak of Heaven —   85
God is Love — and therefore God is Life.   121
God is the center that reconciles the world   94
God is the One, He alone is...   101
God is Truth, hence consequentiality: 260
God repented that He had made man;   273
God says "yes" — the yes of His Reality...   292
God will not ask thee   212
God, the World, the Spirit...   228
God; the prophet; my "I." ...   28
God's morning: when the sun rises   299
God's Truth radiates beauty —   106
God's Word is like the globe of the earth: 57
God-consciousness — hast thou really...   181
God-remembrance is firstly the truth   232
God-remembrance must change man,   157
Good behavior is not for others —   175
Gross manifestation in the outward...   33
Guru is Brahma — says a sacred adage   181
Gypsy violinists, bards and minstrels,   174
Gypsy, thy violin wept a long time —   93
Hades was the dark unknown —   147
Hair-splitting about the nature of God   65
Haphazardness amongst haphazard things —   86
Happy — but not at every moment: 87
Harp and flute — then male and female voices: 150
Have you seen how the soap bubble   61
He is the Truth, the whole Truth...   238
Here-below and hereafter...   6
Him whom thou reverest, fear;...   86
Hinduism — a spiritual world   296
Hinduism is a whole world;   296
Holiness — this is the first greatness;   308
Hope for salvation — its symbol is the future,   289
Horizontal and vertical. Animals walk...   16
How can one feel joy when one knows   276
How can people, who dwell in a God-given...   195
How is it possible, that, in the midst of life,   261
How is it that God acts in human beings?   101
Human language is a kind of miracle —   260
Human language? Words are too narrow;   311
Humility and generosity, then patience...   207
Humility is self-knowledge — objectivity   259
I am here, where I am. I could be   47
I am in my ninetieth year; I have   217
I am too tired to think of God,   10
I ask not others what Truth   211
I call it exteriorization with a view...   189
I cannot stand within existence   115
I do not criticize the penitent or the ascetic;   64
I do not excuse people who, out of pride,   150
I have lived through a whole century   258
I heard a lute deep in the night —   91
I knew a man — wrote Muhyiddin —   272
I know a man who is ninety years old.   241

I know, I will, I can, I do — 45
I must speak of many different things, 137
I think again and again of how 312
I think, but I do not brood; 27
I was born by a river — 285
I wished to put down my pen 205
I would like to stand before the sun, 8
I-consciousness is a two-edged sword; 66
If I tell you that humility is everything — 207
If one cannot know whether an order 210
If one wants to assess the rebelliousness... 173
If one wishes to walk happily... 254
If something makes thee suffer, then think 25
If something petty annoys and troubles thee, 295
If thou believest in God, believe also in thyself— 273
If thou protect the Lord in thy heart, 120
If thou saw'st the dance of hips and breasts, 42
If thou see'st the beautiful, which enraptures... 18
If thou speakest with God,... 256
If thou standest before God, then do not rebel, 253
If thou thinkest of God, thou canst never... 243
Imagine that thou hast a pain 130
In a time when our world was still dreaming — 188
In a world where all faith is disappearing, 201
In all circumstances, the believer... 225
In all sectors of humanity, there are limits 170
In earthly existence, thou canst not avoid 34
In earthly happenings there are oscillations; 273
In earthly things there is always... 198
In German, there are names like "Gottfried," 216
In God's Essence shines a silent Light 122
In God's Presence: no object 157
In God-remembrance remain far... 72
In Hades there is a river called "Lethe"; 143
In Hindu terms, Christ is an example 90
In India it is said that wise men know God; 163
In India it was the custom among the brahmins 185
In India, it is often said that *Japa-Yoga* 15
In Islam it is said that hell does not last forever, 129
In Islam, music was at first proscribed 102
In Japan, one calls *tomoye* a circle 22
In Japan, *táriki* is the way of 246
In mid-life, the fan is open: 169
In my childhood I prayed: 253
In my childhood, I was told that 195
In my early youth, my salvation was 163
In my youth, I often heard 161
In Nature, and also in man, there are 166
"In old age, everything fades away"... 195
In old age, one does not have much choice; 51
In old age, one has many memories — 162
In pious old songbooks I used to find 170
In principle, every man can become a saint, 186
In Pure Being there was a possibility, 254
In reality, the path to God is not a movement — 121
In the beginning God said: "Let there be light!" 111
In the beginning was the Word. 6
In the church there is holy water, 123
In the early morning sunshine, thou art... 90

"In the early morning" — sang Shankara — 248
In the Face of God, I seek to know nothing — 39
In the guilds of earlier times 129
In the idea that God is one 282
In the *krita-yuga*, space was so wide, 68
In the noble thou findest renunciation, 271
In the picture book of thought... 225
In the range of all possible thoughts 145
In the West I saw Indians riding, 93
In the West, one calls "philosopher" 246
In the word dwells something of the thing... 292
In this life, unjust opinions 263
In this world, the pious man carries God's grace; 57
In this world, there is always something... 306
India is Shankara together with Vedanta — 98
Inspiration comes — the writing is easy; 62
Is it not strange how the smallest of things 64
Is it not strange that in Antiquity 24
Is it not strange that to beauty 114
Is not *Samprasâda* the highest good? 180
Islam has three formulations which should 229
It can happen that someone prays... 208
It has been said that there is no greater sin 103
It is a pity that one persists in 133
It is astonishing how the manner... 27
It is important, not only that thou believest... 147
It is in God's nature to manifest Himself, 209
It is lamentable that so many people 135
It is man's deepest substance 152
It is natural that the wicked enemy 210
It is not astonishing that the evil one... 236
It is not good that Adam be alone, 220
It is not true that old people are spiritually... 285
It is often difficult to remain in the Eternal, 212
It is often said that even in evil... 132
It is often said that the joy of love 297
It is related that the Messenger of God 207
It is remarkable how many animals... 300
It is said of a pseudo-philosopher — 134
It is said that fear alone maintains the world — 25
It is said that ye should hold firmly onto forms; 74
It is said: in pain shall woman give birth; 25
It is said: the morning hour has gold... 294
It is said: wisdom is to know 100
It is strange how small things can give us joy — 170
It is strange that in brave peoples' 76
It is strange that we must plod through life — 298
It is taught that sociology is everything — 303
It is very difficult to bear absurdity; 309
It may be that there are now enough songs — 228
It may happen that our joy in the Most High 228
It might be asked whether we have a right 182
It might be asked why it is permissible for me 167
It must be so: there are the different religions — 148
It seems contradictory that a man 278
It will pass — how often canst thou say this! 147
It would be wrong to think that music 218
Joy in multiplicity and joy in unity — 194
Just as the Lord radiated the world 100

Just as the stars glimmer in the abyss of night, 236
Just as, with warmth, ice becomes water, 59
Kaleidoscope — a children's toy, 131
Killing is impossible for the *brahmana*; 82
Krishna and Christ are two poles of the Spirit: 99
Krishna saw his own self — as the Infinite — 99
Krishna stands in the center. Upon him gaze 222
Leave behind thoughts that plague thee... 140
Let me greet the deep and wild forest — 12
Let not thyself be troubled by the phantoms 47
Let the dead bury their dead, 132
Leucippus, Democritus, and other dreamers 219
Life — a mixture of good and bad; 310
Life is not like a picture book 255
Life without happenings does not exist — 230
Life, it is said, is a movement towards death; 119
"Light comes from the East" — this is true, 217
Livest thou in space? This must be somewhere; 75
Logic is right thinking. But not only this — 296
Look not, dreaming, into the past 245
Look to the future, not to false hopes; 157
Love is not mere sentimental play, 41
Love, indifference, scorn, hatred — 309
Love, it is said, lasts only for a time — 42
Lower *Māyā* is materiality: 294
Mā shā'a 'Llāh — Allāh karīm — 77
Man arose from God's creative power; 67
Man can perceive the whole world, 257
Man can speak, and so make the inward... 151
Man does not belong entirely to this earth; 289
Man has a brain in order to think; 161
Man is a mixture of luminosity and heaviness — 290
Man is created to be a god, 140
Man is half animal, half angel;... 256
Man is like a tree in a river. 231
Man is made not only of proud power 196
Man is nostalgia for Paradise 91
Man is not only thinking, he is also willing, 311
Man is the image of God, but the Lord 102
Man is the likeness of God: 70
Man lives because he has been born — 284
Man needs canonical prayer — 36
"Man proposes and God disposes," ... 213
Man wants life and he flees the naught; 194
Man's happiness is his peace of soul. 244
Man's knowledge — it must have limits; 88
Many are of the opinion that an idea... 175
Many people, both male and female, 69
Mary is the image of the seven sorrows; 29
Māyā is a greater enigma than *Ātmā,* 221
Melancholy, despair, hatred and bitterness, 85
Men have difficulty in understanding 301
Men who have no true center 144
Mental images can be like houses 175
Mere appearance and reality 295
Metaphysics — what is one supposed to know? 77
Metaphysics speaks of final things 38
Metaphysics, said a Jesuit, 38
Mighty is the pulse-beat of the Godhead, 198

Miserable are philosophers 149
Monks in West and East sings Psalms 269
Monks too know about matrimonial duties; 269
Motionless center, outside time, 111
Mount Meru, it is said, is the center 94
My first homeland was the Germanic... 62
My late father, who played the violin in Oslo, 270
Mystery of patience: the sorrow and vexation 29
Naïve expressions often carry a deep meaning; 27
Necessity and accidence: these are 290
Neti, neti — "not this, not this" — why cannot 48
No man is saved without the Mercy 243
Noble mentality and correct behavior 197
Non-Being: this is synonymous with... 119
Not only revelation, but also experience... 6
Number is without limit, it grows and swells; 33
O beata Solitudo, O sola Beatitudo — 262
O man, remain what thou art; do not seek, 240
O Nightingale, what sings thy flute, 266
Obligation is compulsion... 11
Of humility I have often spoken — 213
Of what does the "I" consist? Firstly, ... 46
Often thou hast fought the past — 147
Old men, they say, are of sad disposition; 11
Om namo sarva Tathāgata Om — 49
On doomsday, it is said, men tremble, 50
On the one hand, meditation: 116
On this poor earth, greatness demands 127
One can be so objective, without prejudice 138
One can endlessly torment oneself... 12
One could talk endlessly of beauty, 302
One day follows the next, and man 232
One God and He alone; then the Prophets 169
One kind of God-remembrance is solemn... 113
One knows not whether the world is... 31
One man, one word — think not that... 214
One may call good, from a pious point of view, 160
One may sometimes wonder why God 265
One must beware of sensory and mental... 142
One must speak of little things... 226
One of the things that makes us happiest 41
One says that this or that will give thee joy; 30
One should distinguish between a defect 307
One should never believe in what is past — 144
One should not confuse true virtue 279
One should not fear what the damned one... 303
One should not praise the day... 291
One was afraid of something without reason — 292
One would gladly live without the evil one 117
One would like to soar on high, 162
Only an empty head can be bored — 176
Our life is filled with events, 257
Painters of the Far East love clouds of mist — 71
Palaces, columns, statues, marble staircases — 226
Pandora's box is the potentiality 298
Paradise is the highest value for the soul, 118
Paradise knows no icy cold — 143
Paradox: we are in earthly life 7
Peace and joy are the two poles 105

People do what wears out their spirit, 68
People said that the Red Indians were savages, 216
People with the following prejudices 279
Perhaps the most difficult thing... 230
Poetry, music, and dance — these arts 127
Position in society is one thing, 129
"Praise the Lord" — what does this mean? 118
Prayer — firstly it is commanded; 75
Priest and warrior. The priest is also 278
Principle and manifestation; one could also say: 182
Profundity and strength, richness and joy... 166
Promise not more than thou canst keep; 116
Prose is fresh, unfettered thinking; 34
Rapture or ecstasy: it may differ 200
Reality: God is first, and alone. 115
Reason alone — you see where it leads; 193
Reason, sentiment, imagination and memory: 76
Refuge in God may lie in thy will; 271
Reincarnation — for Hindus and Buddhists 221
Relativity as a theory 134
Relativity: an oft-used 237
Religion — on the one hand it is God, 126
Religion gives us happiness in life, 270
Remembrance of God — thinking of the One; 79
Remembrance of God has two dimensions: 264
Remembrance of God knows no number — 183
Sacred languages: Sanskrit, Hebrew, and 89
Sadness of soul is a ploy of the evil one — 162
Saintly people often have to suffer 191
San Juan de la Cruz warned us 199
Sattva, rajas, tamas: light, heat, heaviness; 301
Say not that man may see God only in trials — 26
Say nothing false, hide nothing true — 310
"Say: God — and leave them to their idle... 287
Science: what counts is not what 133
"Sculptor God, strike me, I am the stone"— 299
Securitas — people are obsessed... 68
See'st thou the rock in the middle of the ocean? 79
Seeing, a priori, is always "towards the outside" 141
Seeming paradises — men who are but... 300
Self-assurance is a fragile thing. 60
Selfishness and vengefulness, and therefore... 171
Self-respect is natural in the noble man, 44
Semites greet with: Peace be with thee! 273
Sensible consolation is valuable for faith; 264
"Sensible consolations," says theology 65
Serenity — without petty conditions; 274
Serenity and Certitude — and likewise: 51
Serenity is Divine Nature; 184
Several lives, but within one life — 105
She, who silences the river of thoughts, 251
Shri Ramakrishna sought to emphasize 245
Since thou dost exist, thou must be someone 84
So many people are but fragments, pieces, 17
So many things has thine active mind... 72
Solitude is the lot of the sage, because 145
Some say that, with God, knowledge 128
Some take their stand on the ground of faith, 130
Some think that he who strives for personal... 295

Somehow nature works better 254
Someone saw the Name of God... 260
Someone was vexed and downcast — 30
Something that did not exist in earlier times 279
Somewhere I read that only he has faith 88
Somewhere in the Bible there is mention 209
South-east Asia — celestial dances 35
Space and time: ether and energy; 256
Space is infinite, and so is time — 111
Space must repeat forms endlessly, 97
Spanish melodies, falling from the lute... 167
Spiritual contemplation, *darshan*, ... 178
"State" and "station" — *hāl, maqām* — 115
Stillness in God — I could sing thy praise 276
Strength of will is not aggressiveness;... 41
Strong is not the one who has banished... 171
Such is the world — worries and sorrows; 159
Suddenly snow came to my forest. 12
Sun, gold, lion, honey, 37
Sunrise: the sun rises in the sky — 293
Take thy refuge in the Lord; 271
That earthly people are what they are, 308
That evil exists 232
That our earth goes round the sun, 141
The ancient East is based on Truth — 40
The angels are the Godhead's faculties 209
The animal does not know that one day... 218
The anticipation — within the proof itself — 168
The Arabs told me: slowness 43
The archetype, breaking through the naught, 113
The ascetic seeks not only to obtain salvation — 183
The *Avatāra* must have two souls: 128
The ball of the sun is a real symbol; 197
The beginning of God-remembrance is silence 270
The *Bhagavad-Gita* — The Song... 215
The *bhakta* loves, but not the *jñāni* — 81
The *Bhakti-Avatāras* possess crowns, 177
The Bible gave precedence to those who plant, 21
The Bible says: In the beginning was the Word. 198
The blasphemer thinks: if God exists, 102
The chain shows us how the forms of existence 16
The chief reason to think of God 164
The Christmas tree that stood in the center — 96
The city of Paris was the love of my youth — 17
The Creator and Savior is Being; 58
The Creator clothed the wide world 112
The dance of the goddess is the manifestation 180
The days flow past, and every hour 230
The devil contrives that even pious people 60
The devil said: I can do everything, 208
The devil wanted to silence the Master — 234
The dignity of a noble man is not superficial; 165
"The dogs bark and the caravan passes" — 241
The eagle feather, a Red Indian said, 19
The earth is spoiled and poisoned — 33
The earthly field is a poor domain. 286
The ego is proof of the Supreme Self; 160
The enemy of a friend cannot be a friend; 235
The essential nature of the Good... 94

The essential thou shouldst always see;   14
The evil one rails against the Most High;   236
The feeling of certitude is not always   211
The feet of the dancer: they move inwards,   151
The fool holds the science of Ātmā...   305
The German ambience — this was...   239
The golden robe of Truth has two sides: 176
The good, it has been said, is an absolute;   31
The greatest miracle that the angels work   62
The Greek meander represents life,   15
The hands of man manifest his heart;   35
The heart is made of Truth   84
"The heart of the fool is in the house of joy,"   158
"The heart of the wise is in the house"...   157
The Heavens are segments — from rim...   32
The hereafter is not worldly, people say,   43
The Highest Word is not hair-splitting —   179
The immense river of the whole Veda   22
The imperfection of things,   190
The Kalki-Avatāra, it is written,   49
The Kingdom of God is distant,...   85
The Lord certainly does not demand   309
The Lord is completely free — it has been said — 61
The Lord is my shepherd; I shall not want.   207
The Lord is my sufficiency, it is written,   244
The Lord is our refuge — there is no   214
The master of ceremonies of a prince told me: 288
The Master, a voice from the Absolute,   304
The Master, they say, is a superman;   44
The Master, they say, is falsely informed —   234
The meadows are strewn with flowers —   238
The men of olden times were wonderful —   272
The Messenger of God is the whole world —   200
The mild summer night descended upon me —   178
The most beautiful thing that the senses...   70
The naïvety of former times...   122
The Name "All-Merciful" must be...   311
The object of worship is one thing;   96
The oneness of the Most High resounds...   282
"The Opening" — Islam's main prayer —   98
The pariah — an unhappy mixture   265
The penguin wanted a flying contest...   272
The presence of God — this is one thing;   220
The problem of exaggeration: a learned man   160
The radiant green of meadows, bushes, trees —   190
The realm of gnosis is like the starry heavens — 247
The river: a path from non-existence to the All; 104
The saint can work miracles. How   83
The saint, the sage, the hero and   82
The same thing can never repeat itself: 97
The saving Name, invocation and faith: 268
The scales of God thou canst not understand;   34
The sense of the great is an ideal —   307
The sexual parts — in the West they are...   124
The six essential themes of meditation,   271
The soul is a cup whose content   227
The soul is woven of a thousand questions;   88
The soul must become accustomed...   194
The soul needs light from above,   241
The soul of a Sufi came to God;   281
The soul should base itself on thoughts   160
The soul that has become wise   87
"The Spirit is willing, but the flesh is weak":   178
The spirit, the soul — quite often a to-and-fro, 89
The Spirit-Wheel: a symbol in the region   19
The stream of songs already wished to stop;   109
The strength of the bad, the weakness...   26
The substance of the saint is nobility   199
The Sufis distinguish between jadhb, attraction, 262
The Sufis, even more than the Christians,   125
The Supreme Name brings the Truth   246
The swan, the water lily on the pond;   223
The thinking of Germanic people is concrete —   239
The town of Mostaghanem: dark blue sea,   18
The tree grew up from root to crown;   297
The tribes of the tropical forest have religions, 36
The True and the Beautiful are ready   208
The true sage is a sacrament,   235
The truth, the whole truth, and nothing but...   114
The universe is a measureless book   22
The unnatural is also natural,   136
The vehicle — in the world — of the Absolute   304
The Virgen del Pilar possesses a robe   139
The Virgin said: they have no wine.   104
The Virgin: "clothed with the sun alone,"   63
The voice of the folk-song bears witness...   174
The warrior on the battlefield must not flee;   215
The wheel of time turns. All things must move,   63
The white man's starting point is clear thinking, 23
The wise man does not need to choose...   244
The world exists — but as a changing play;   95
The world is a play of enigmas...   308
The world is crooked, but stand thou upright...   61
The world is full of injustices   307
The world is like the vast starry space,   177
The world is made of contradictions —   190
The world of images, which disappears   227
The world-wheel turns, and mocks thee —   215
The worst man is not the shudra,   263
The youth who loves a noble maiden   290
Theodicy — it is a two-edged sword...   185
There are different degrees of union   115
There are many people who praise...   276
There are many things which are indifferent —   274
"There are more things in Heaven and on earth"   287
There are rare people, who as children   139
There are seekers who know too much,   193
There are so many people who love to listen   60
There are three kinds of giving: the first   131
There are two things no one can take from us: 291
There have been mystics who behaved badly —   158
There is a difference between Reality...   180
There is a mysticism of love, which lives...   124
There is a river called the soul —   78
There is an ocean of Māyā surrounding us —   282
"There is no duty higher than Truth" —   303
There is no mass without energy;   32
There is no need to describe water   9

"There is no victor except God":   105
There is the drunkenness of the noble...   299
There is the theory that all things   220
There is the treacherous certitude   283
There was a child whose toy was broken —   17
There were some priests who scolded a yogi: 100
They built for me a beautiful wooden house   66
Things past — of what use are they still?   13
Things, which may or may not be —   166
Think of God as the In-Itself. And then: 99
Thinking lives from what is real;   306
Thou art Benares, said Shri Shankara —   247
Thou canst not always avoid the absurdity...   219
Thou canst not fill a cup that is full —   146
Thou findest world-negation...   80
Thou goest from one dwelling-place to another,   75
Thou grievest over injustice which,   152
Thou hast said God's Name a thousand times,   146
Thou hesitatest before the sword...   131
Thou hurriest along a path following thy desire;   8
Thou livest in this world, not in the next;   51
Thou shouldst not blame the evening...   291
Thou shouldst not cling obstinately...   103
Three kinds of attraction: upward, horizontal...   255
Three times Greece had a particular greatness: 223
Time of youth — already past and gone —   92
Time, people say, becomes ever shorter   275
To be "I" is to relate all things   112
To err is human, but to persevere in error   284
To exist, is to be such and such. If you exist,   275
To God belong the most beautiful Names,   244
To know that, whatever happens,   282
To most people, it seems obvious   164
To receive is good, if it is not egoism —   191
To see the Lord in everything means: 167
To the extent that thou believest...   313
To think is natural; unnatural   28
Trials are purifications that come from God —   208
Trust in thy good star —   308
Truth gives the spirit deep peace;   221
Truth is everything. Altruism is   10
Truth is not always what one wishes.   288
Truths that do not change   146
Two doors has the earthly life of man: 49
Two entirely different things are man as such   227
Two opposites: wisdom and woman —   225
Two poles: metaphysics and music;   225
Two values are consoling — I wish to say...   140
Understand that within love dwell beauty   174
Uninterrupted by the wheel of time,   65
Unitive thought and separative thought: 172
Upward: the way to Heaven   168
Vacare Deo — then involvement with things: 274
Vairāgya — equanimity and serenity,   50
Vairāgya — equanimity. Because what is...   248
Vertical line and horizontal line —   16
Vishnu and Lakshmi — lofty powers   122
Warmth pertains to light;   284
We are in this world to manifest   139

We came to sing about God.   87
We distinguish between a place and Infinity;   187
We distinguish between two kinds of ugliness: 73
We do not believe what is true...   136
We do not criticize the good missionary   149
We live in time; who can rest?   86
What counts in life? It is that thou avoidest   218
What distinguishes a butterfly   45
What does epistemology seek to explain?   193
What does the *Mea Culpa* mean?   10
What God has given thee...   13
What I give to God — it is prefigured   89
What I think and what I am,   72
What in Sanskrit is called *tamas*,   130
What is evil? Not a second being,   114
"What is exaggerated is insignificant" —   277
What is greatness in men? When genius   93
What is it that makes man miserable?   40
What is nobility of soul...   26
What is the difference between earth...   92
What is the I — who has woven this dream   302
What is valid for the macrocosm,   188
What makes man happy? Prayer;   268
What makes thee completely happy?...   79
What matters is not — some have said —   101
What paradises are — one knows well;   21
What the Indians call *wakan*, or   224
What the spirit and the heart teach us   159
What this earthly life is,   312
What was the cloud in which Enoch...   196
What we are, we are through God's Will;   277
What we call Spirit is first and foremost...   228
What, in my youth, was cruelly real,   145
When an experience — be it of beauty...   140
When an intelligent man   267
When Christ spoke against long prayers,   192
When did stillness lay itself upon the song?   139
When God decides to send a being...   233
When God's Name resounds in thy...   112
When looking at something, what counts...   281
When man turns to God, the evil enemy   233
When one combines the All with the naught,   9
When one has wandered through nearly...   219
When one is not directly engaged in prayer —   159
When passion is combined with profundity,   40
When people engage in something shameful   150
When several people share the same destiny,   235
When the soil was fertile,   19
When thou directest thy steps, O man,   121
When you call upon the Lord...   280
Where does the path of science lead?   15
Where there is light, there must also be shadow.   152
Where wilt thou dwell in eternity?   48
Whether I be here below, or above   113
Whether one be eight or eighty —   259
Whether or not one may say something ugly?   74
Which would be better, one might ask,   212
Who is greater: the one who is perfectly holy,   195
Who is the "I" of the ray of Revelation?   210

Who may be the origin of a trial?   238
Whoever says *Ātmā*, must think of *Māyā*;   283
Whom God unites, let no man put asunder,   42
Why are these songs without names?   3
Why did Shankara, the sage, like to compare   265
Why did the Red Indians always fight...   23
Why is hell compared with fire?   142
Why is *Māyā* so lavish,   213
Why lovest thou, O soul, from time to time,   36
Why repeat things endlessly?   39
Why should I not revere the sun?   127
Why was Solomon so misunderstood?   11
Why wast thou moved by gypsy violins,   37
Wisdom and faith are considered opposites —   304
With David, Krishna and Shankara...   269

With sacred formulas — mantras...   123
With the rising of the sun comes the day —   233
With what wilt thou replace the river...   231
Within my heart the weary day is singing —   118
World-murderers I would call those fools   142
Ye ask for proof of the Highest Being,   92
Ye ask: can religion be a homeland?   58
Ye may be astonished that in the mysticism   128
Ye think of times when miracles occurred;   189
Ye think that there are human collectivities,   5
You ask me how the soul should be molded   9
You ask what may the hero mean for us —   83
You must understand the troubadours aright —   192
Youthful beauty is a two-edged sword;   241
Zeus made the *panta rhei* — the flowing   231

Books by Frithjof Schuon

The Transcendent Unity of Religions
Spiritual Perspectives and Human Facts
Gnosis: Divine Wisdom
Language of the Self
Stations of Wisdom
Understanding Islam
Light on the Ancient Worlds
In the Tracks of Buddhism
Treasures of Buddhism
Logic and Transcendence
Esoterism as Principle and as Way
Castes and Races
Sufism: Veil and Quintessence
From the Divine to the Human
Christianity/Islam: Essays on Esoteric Ecumenicism
Survey of Metaphysics and Esoterism
In the Face of the Absolute
The Feathered Sun: Plains Indians in Art and Philosophy
To Have a Center
Roots of the Human Condition
Images of Primordial and Mystic Beauty: Paintings by Frithjof Schuon
Echoes of Perennial Wisdom
The Play of Masks
The Transfiguration of Man
The Eye of the Heart
Form and Substance in the Religions

Edited Writings of Frithjof Schuon

The Essential Writings of Frithjof Schuon, ed. Seyyed Hossein Nasr
The Fullness of God: Frithjof Schuon on Christianity,
ed. James S. Cutsinger
Prayer Fashions Man: Frithjof Schuon on the Spiritual Life,
ed. James S. Cutsinger
Art from the Sacred to the Profane: East and West
ed. Catherine Schuon

Poetry by Frithjof Schuon

Sulamith, Berna, Urs Graf Verlag, 1946

Tage- und Nächtebuch, Berna, Urs Graf Verlag, 1946

The Garland, Abodes, 1994

Road to the Heart: Poems, World Wisdom Books, 1995

Liebe, Verlag Herder Freiburg im Breisgau, 1997

Leben, Verlag Herder Freiburg im Breisgau, 1997

Glück, Verlag Herder Freiburg im Breisgau, 1997

Sinn, Verlag Herder Freiburg im Breisgau, 1997

Amor y Vida. Poesías, Mallorca, José J. de Olañeta, Editor, 1999

Sinngedigchte/Poésies didactiques, Volumes 1-10,
Sottens, Suisse, Editions Les Sept Flèches, 2000-2005

Songs for a Spiritual Traveler: Selected Poems, World Wisdom, 2001

Adastra & Stella Maris: Poems by Frithjof Schuon, World Wisdom, 2003

Autumn Leaves & The Ring: Poems by Frithjof Schuon, World Wisdom, 2007

Songs without Names: Volumes I-VI, World Wisdom, 2006

Songs without Names: Volumes VII-XII, World Wisdom, 2006

World Wheel: Volumes I-III, World Wisdom, 2006

World Wheel: Volumes IV-VII, World Wisdom, 2006